nurtured futility - volume one : the new violence

the new violence • nihil 1 • 2011

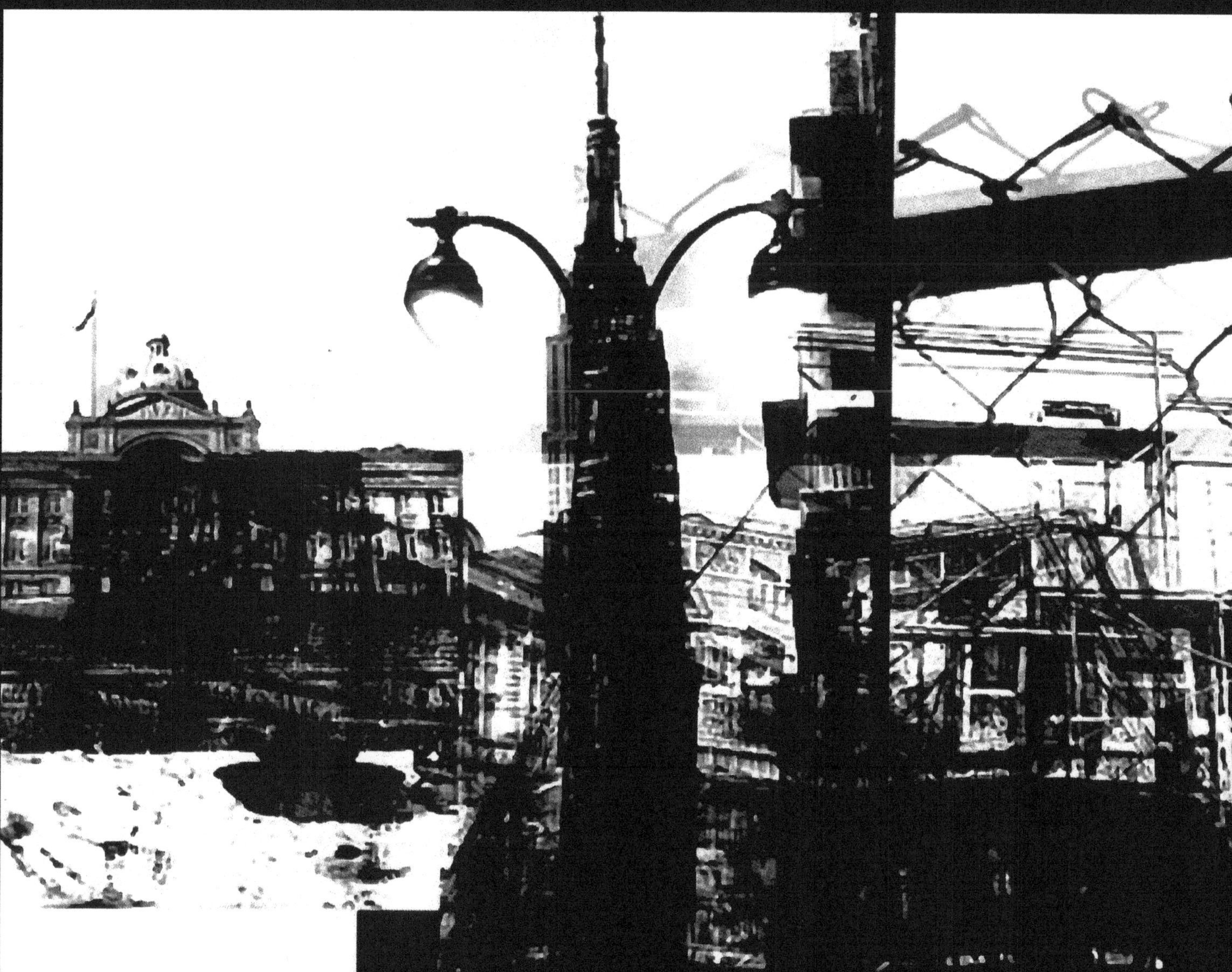

A Farewell Note to this City

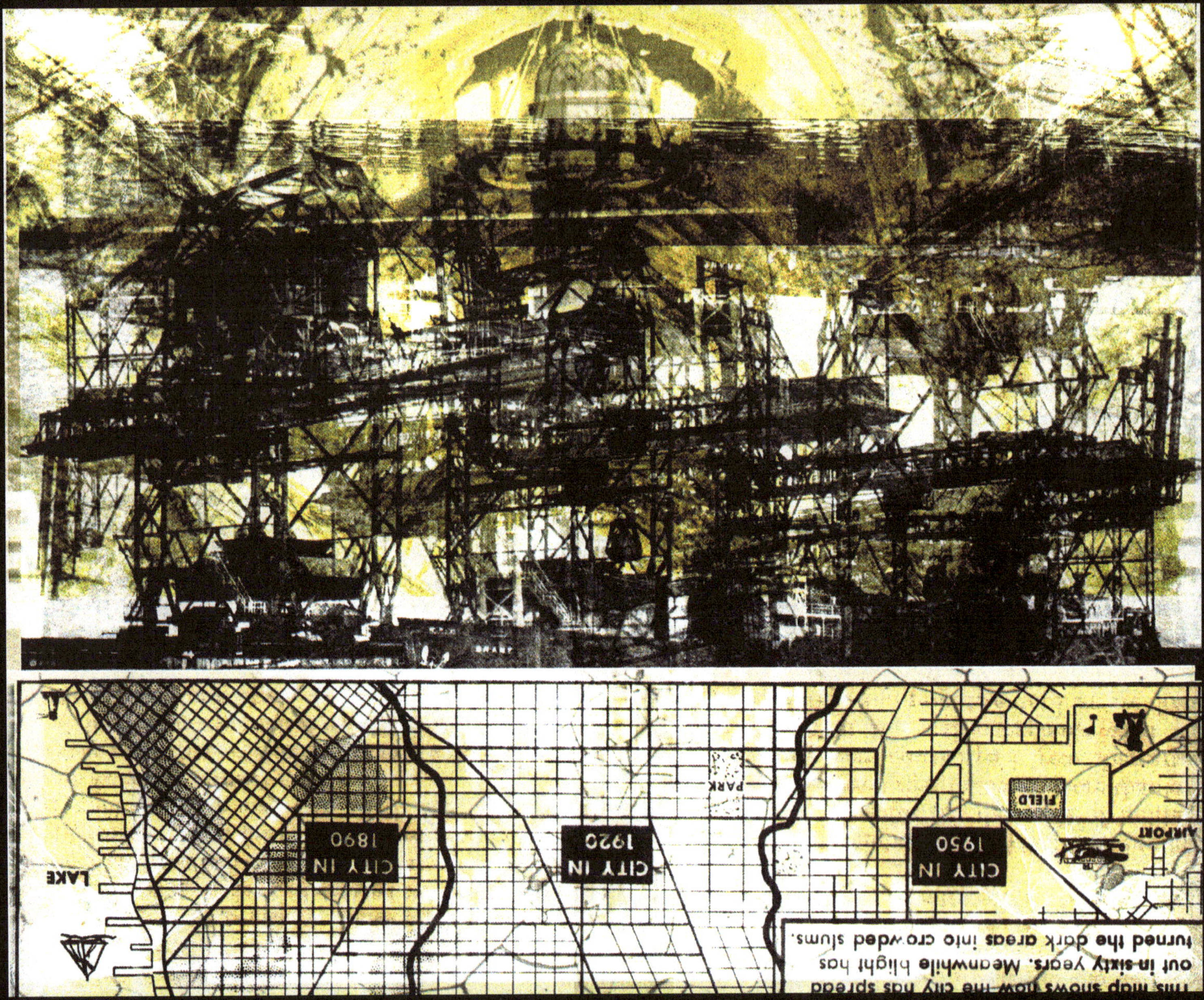

Breadwinner

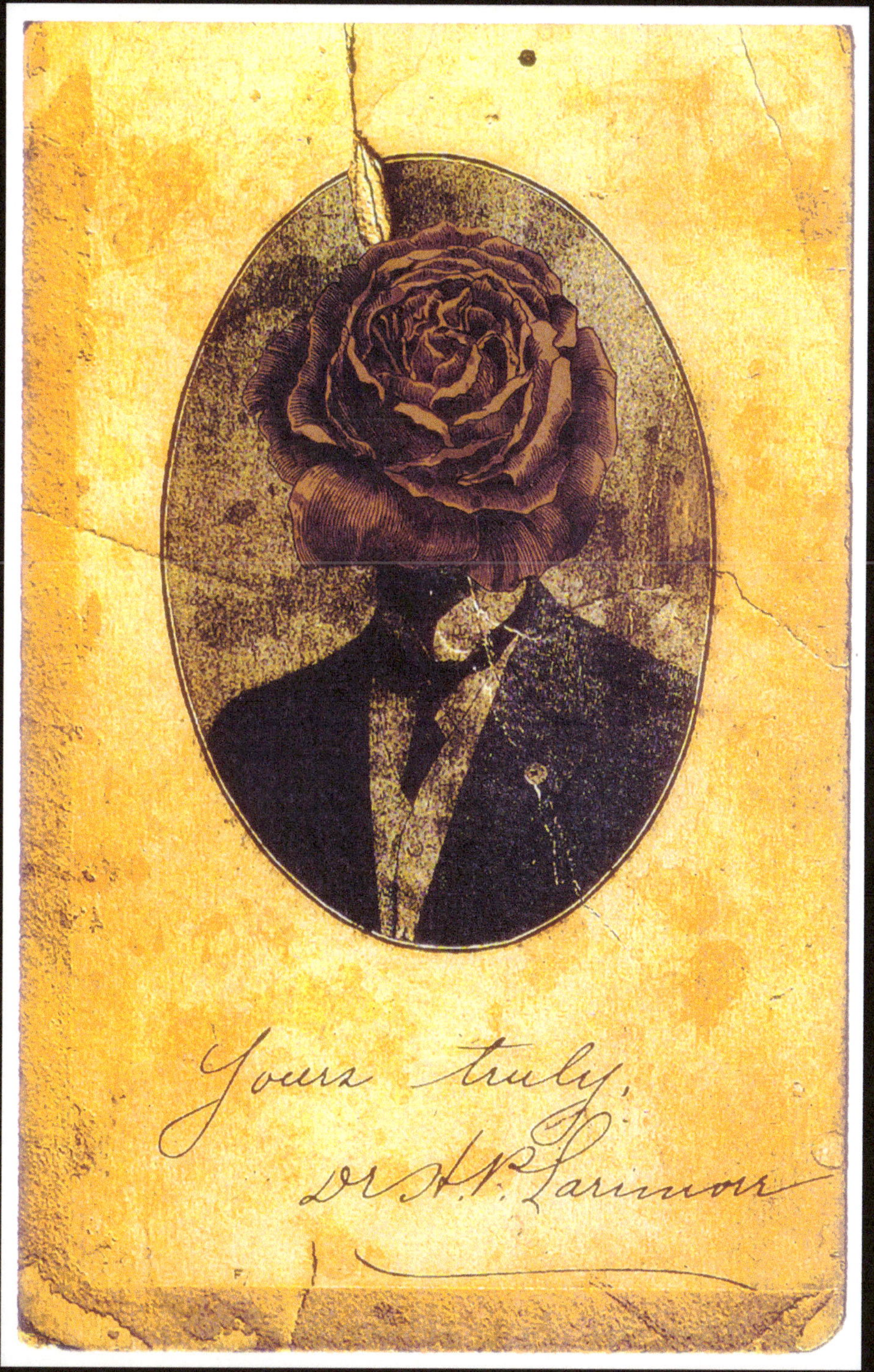
Yours truly,

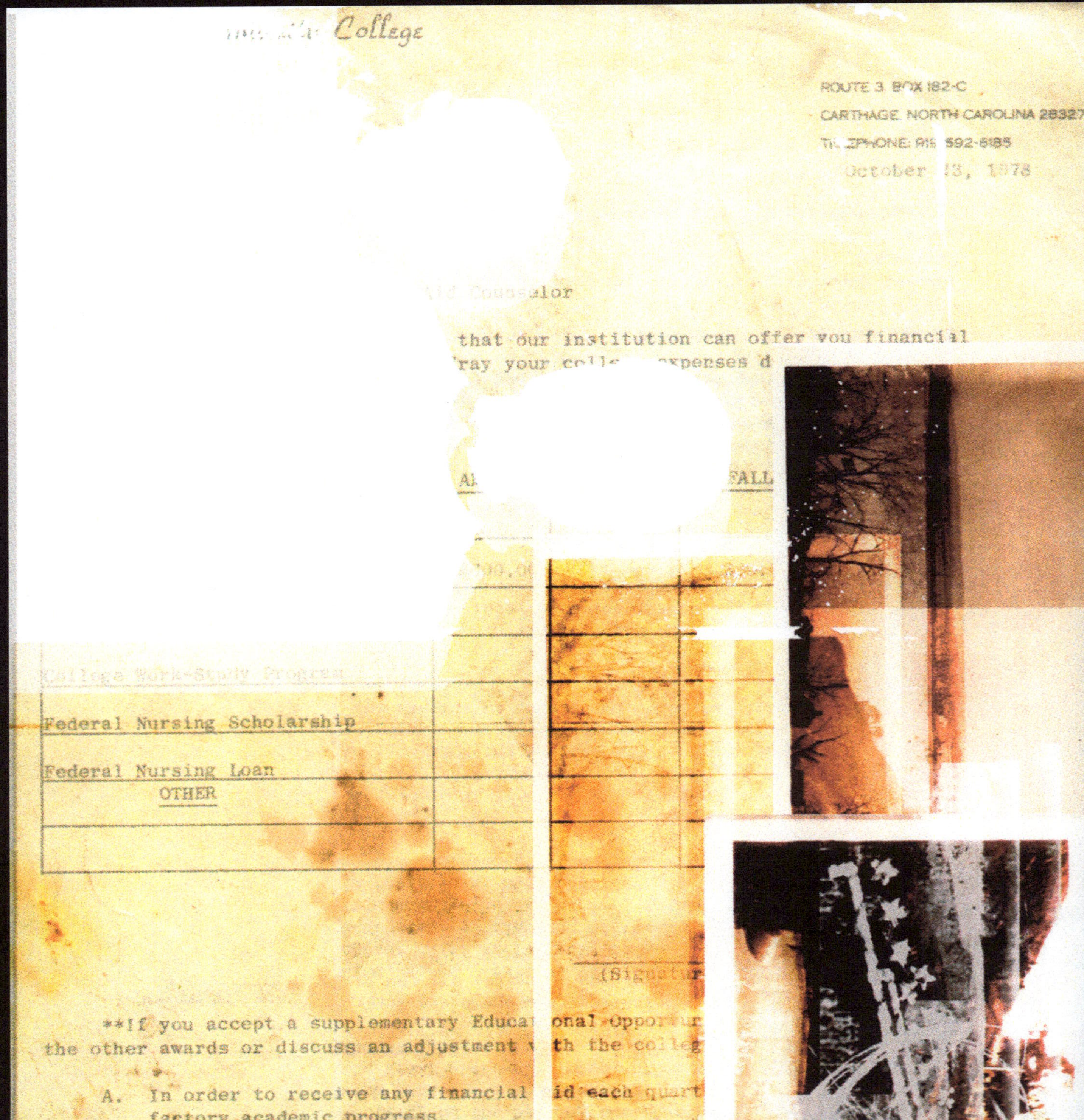
College
ROUTE 3 BOX 182-C
CARTHAGE NORTH CAROLINA 28327
October 13, 1978
Counselor
that our institution can offer you financial
ray your colle expenses d
FALL
College Work-Study Program
Federal Nursing Scholarship
Federal Nursing Loan
OTHER
**If you accept a supplementary Educa onal Oppor
the other awards or discuss an adjustment th the colleg
A. In order to receive any financial id each quart

Beating Me at My Own Game

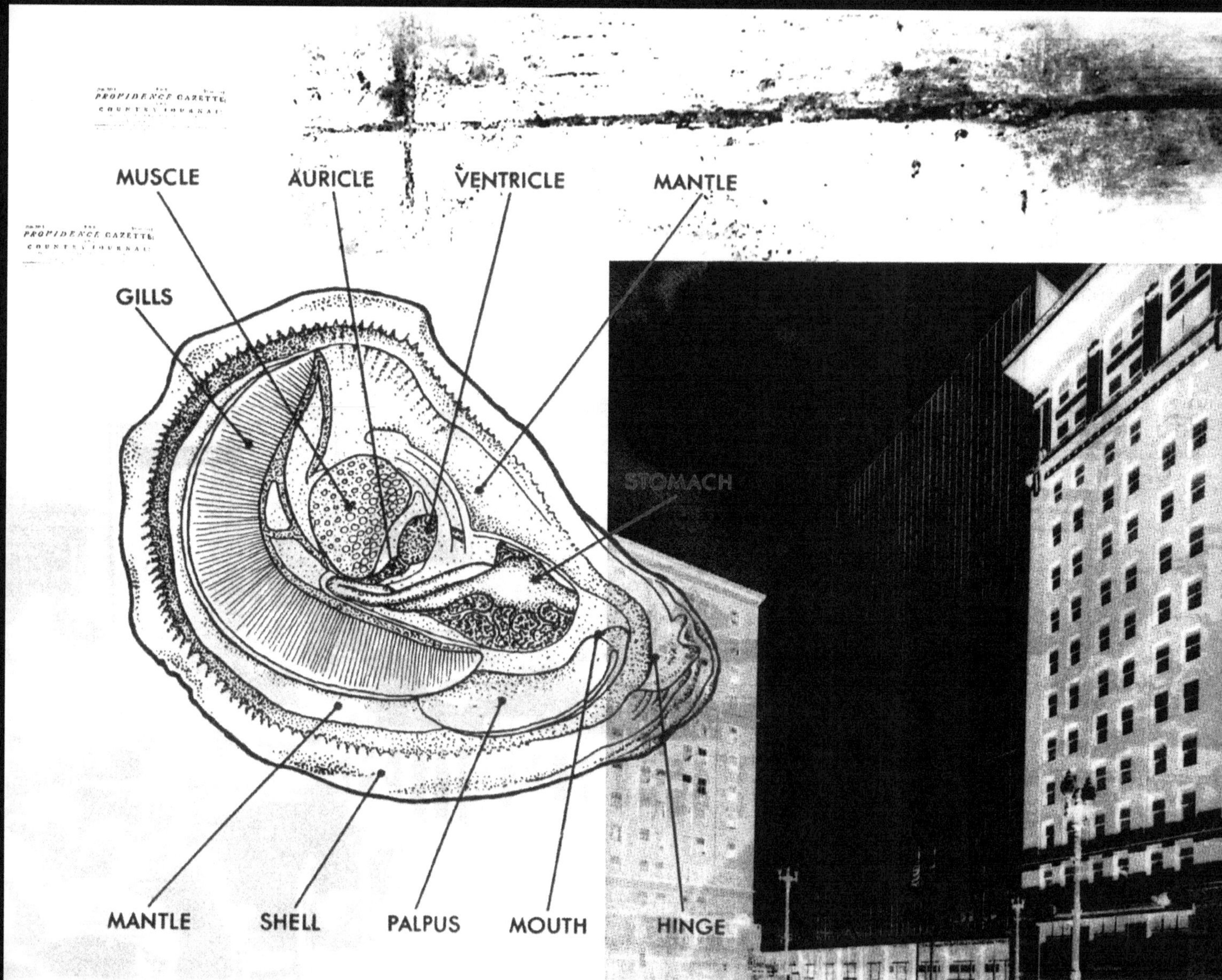

Christopher Walken's Autograph

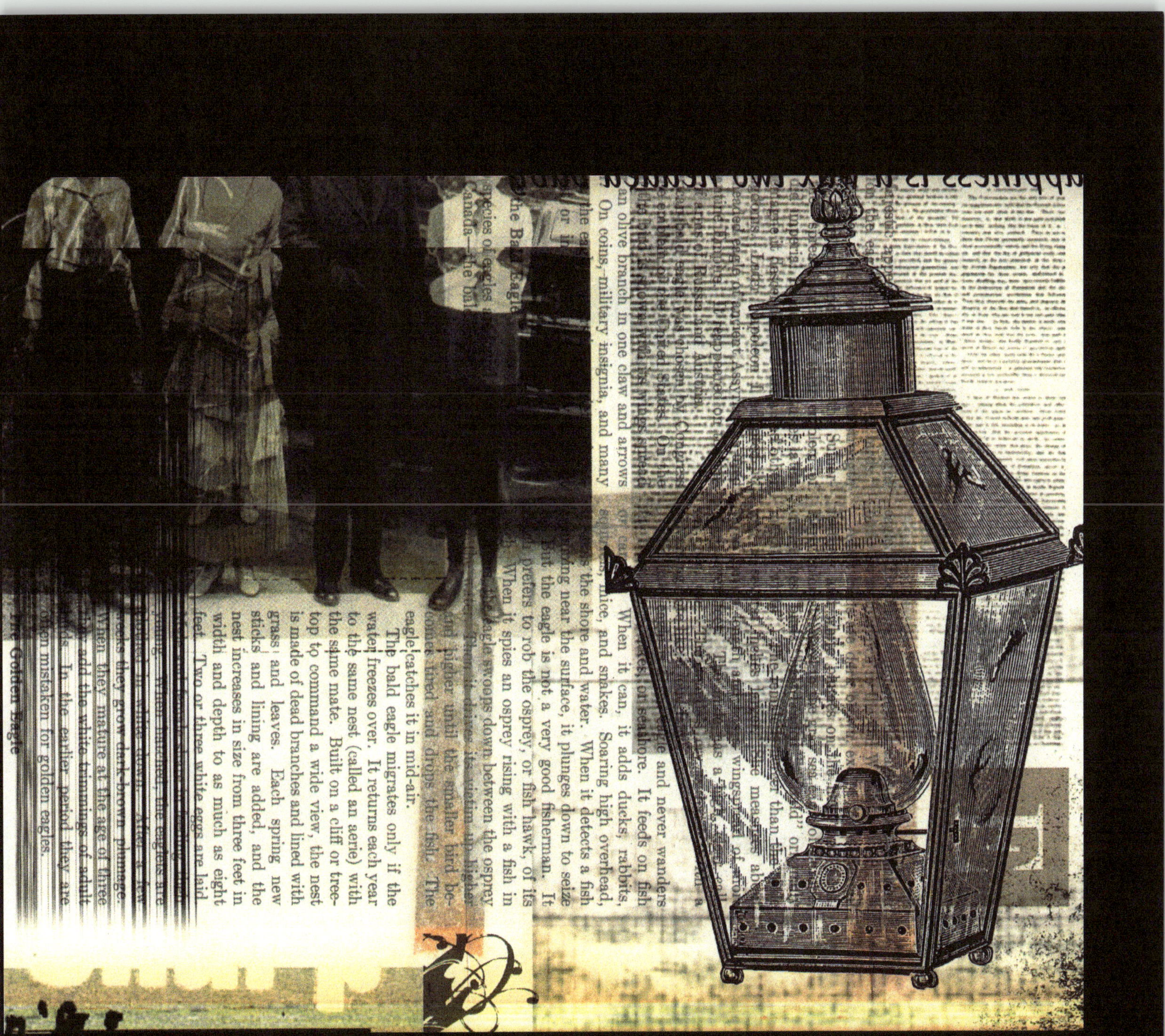

Happiness is a Wax Two-headed Baby

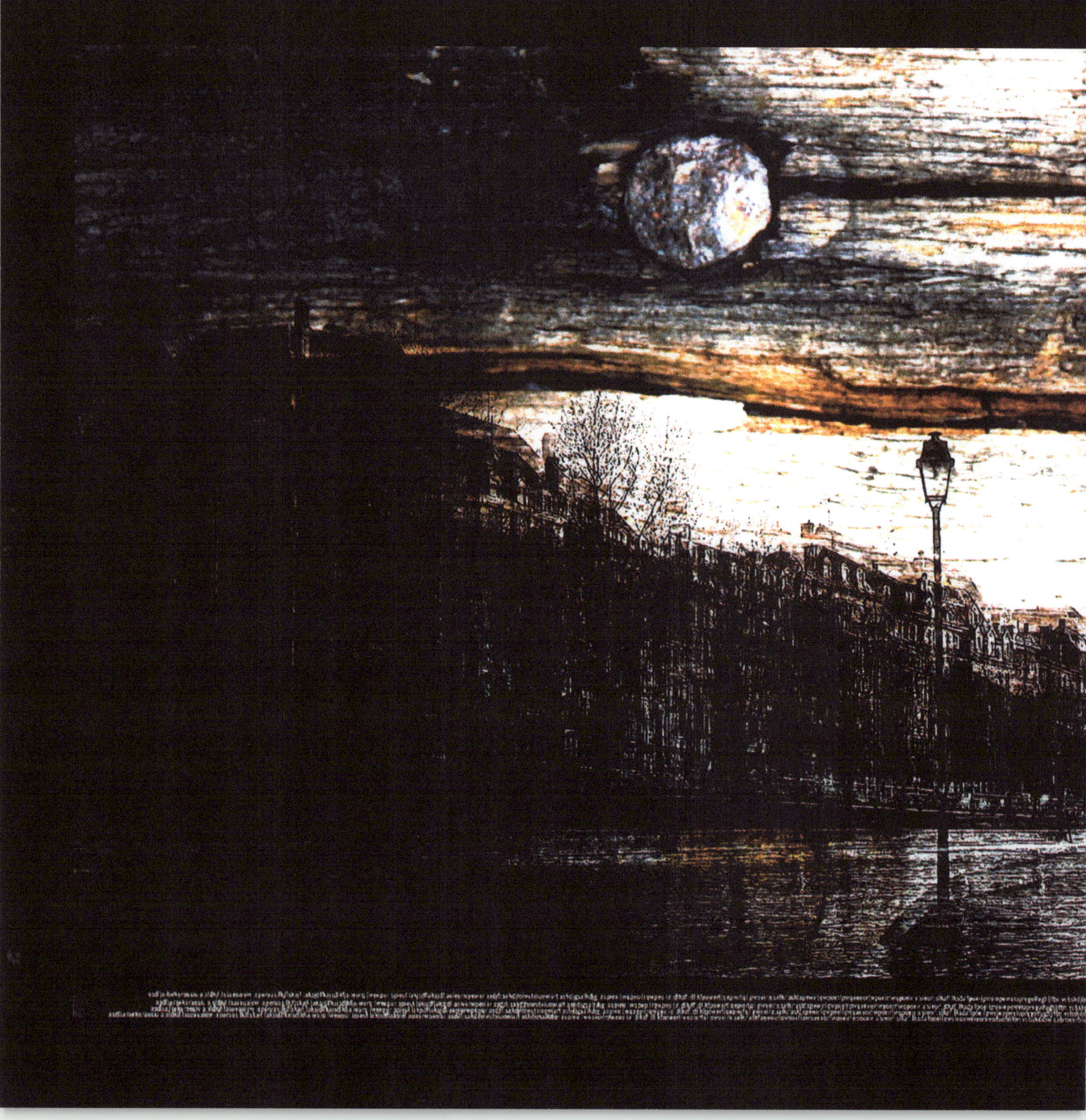

A Farewell Note to this City II

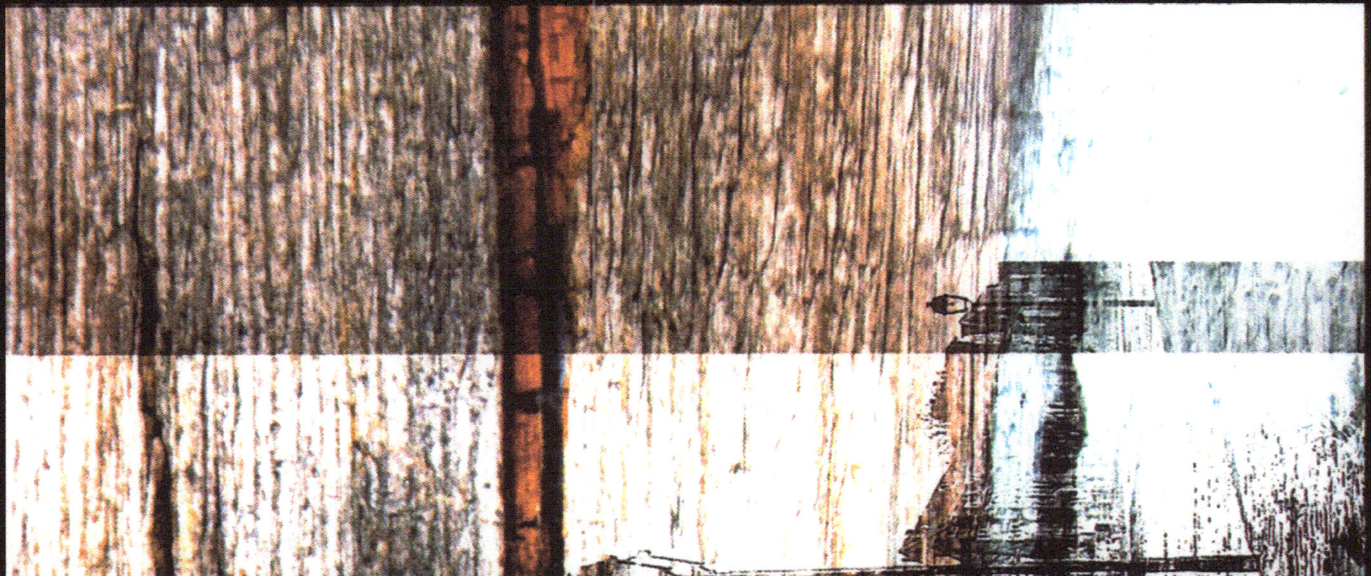

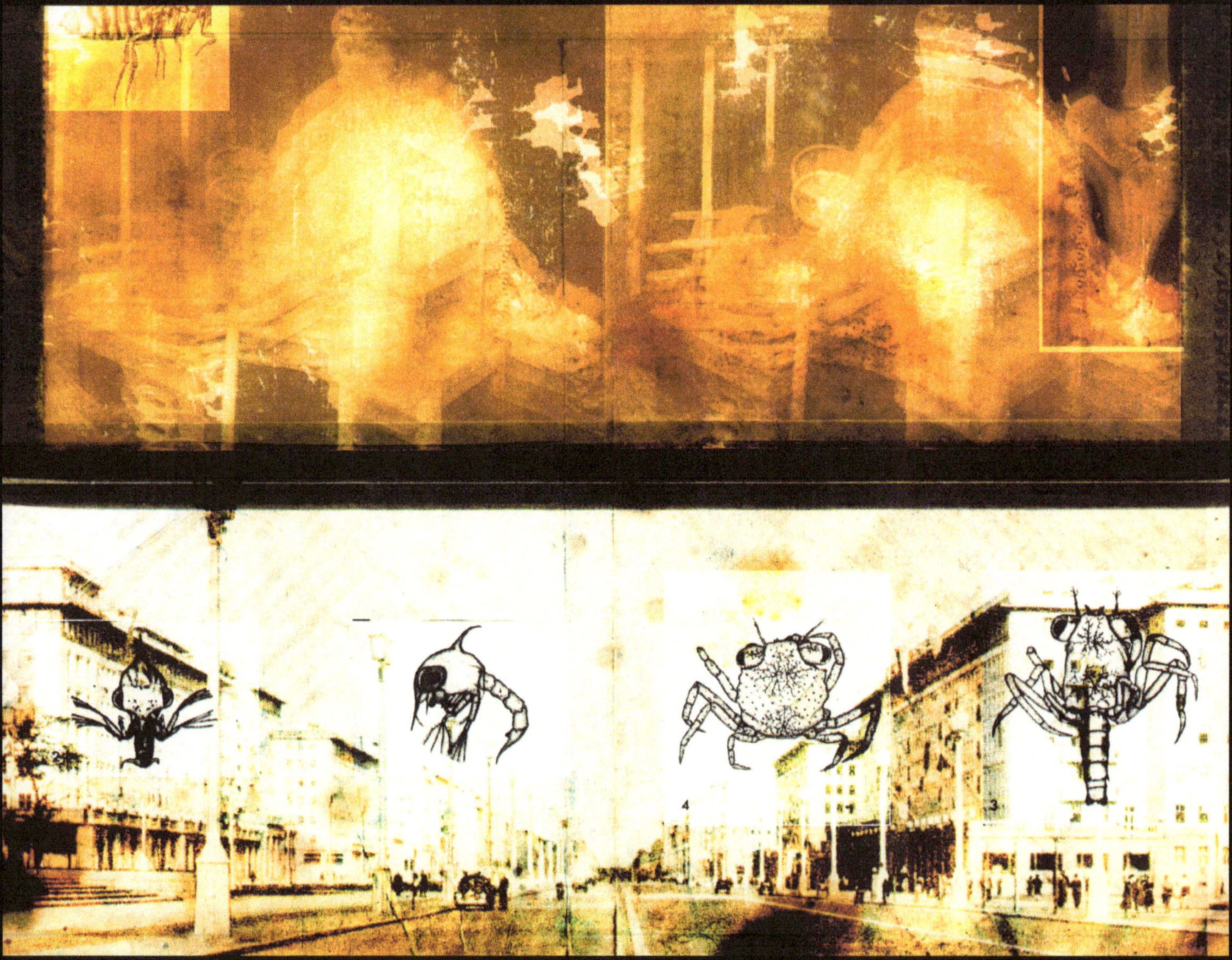

Amalgamation Station

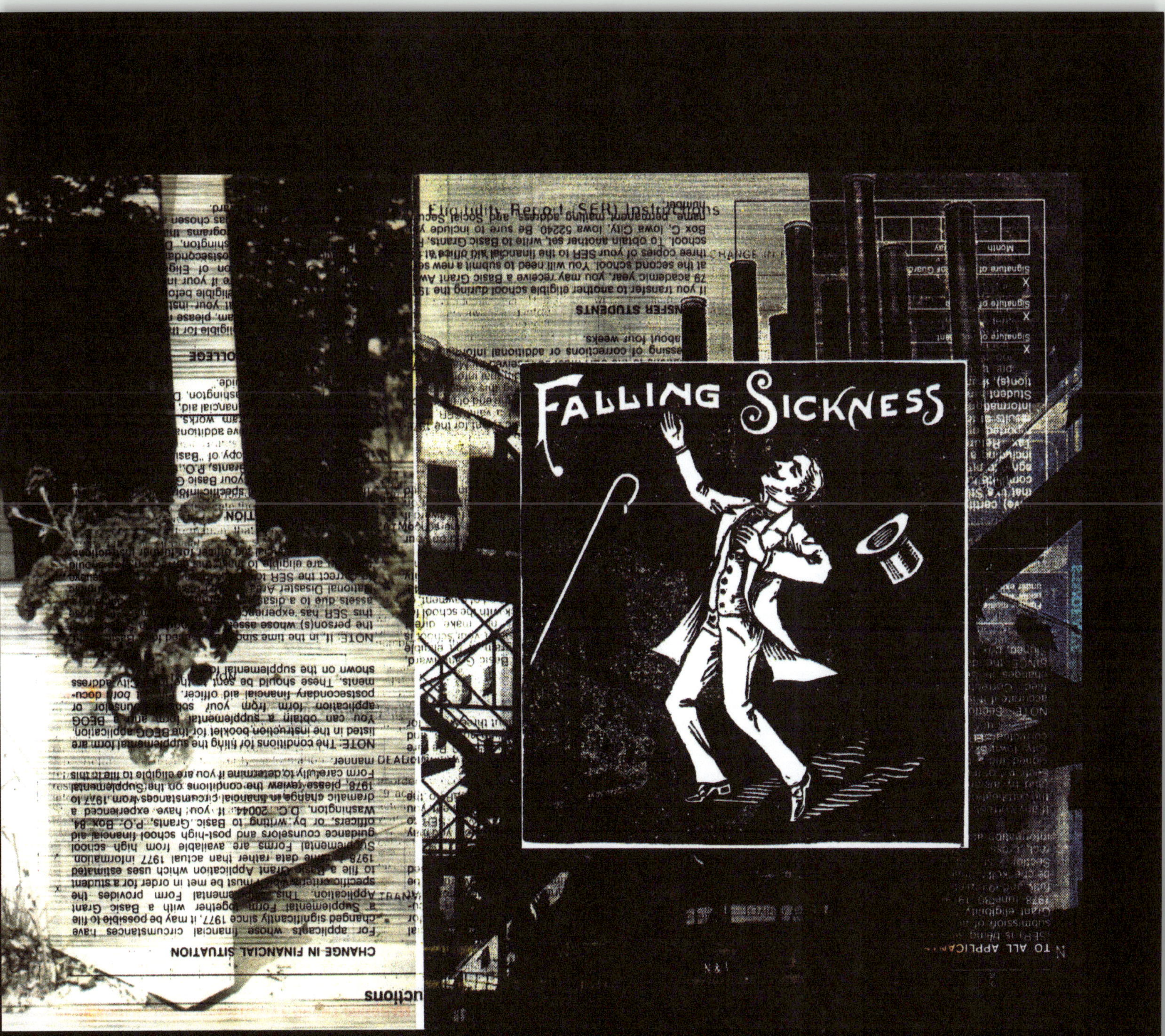

Heretic-tock

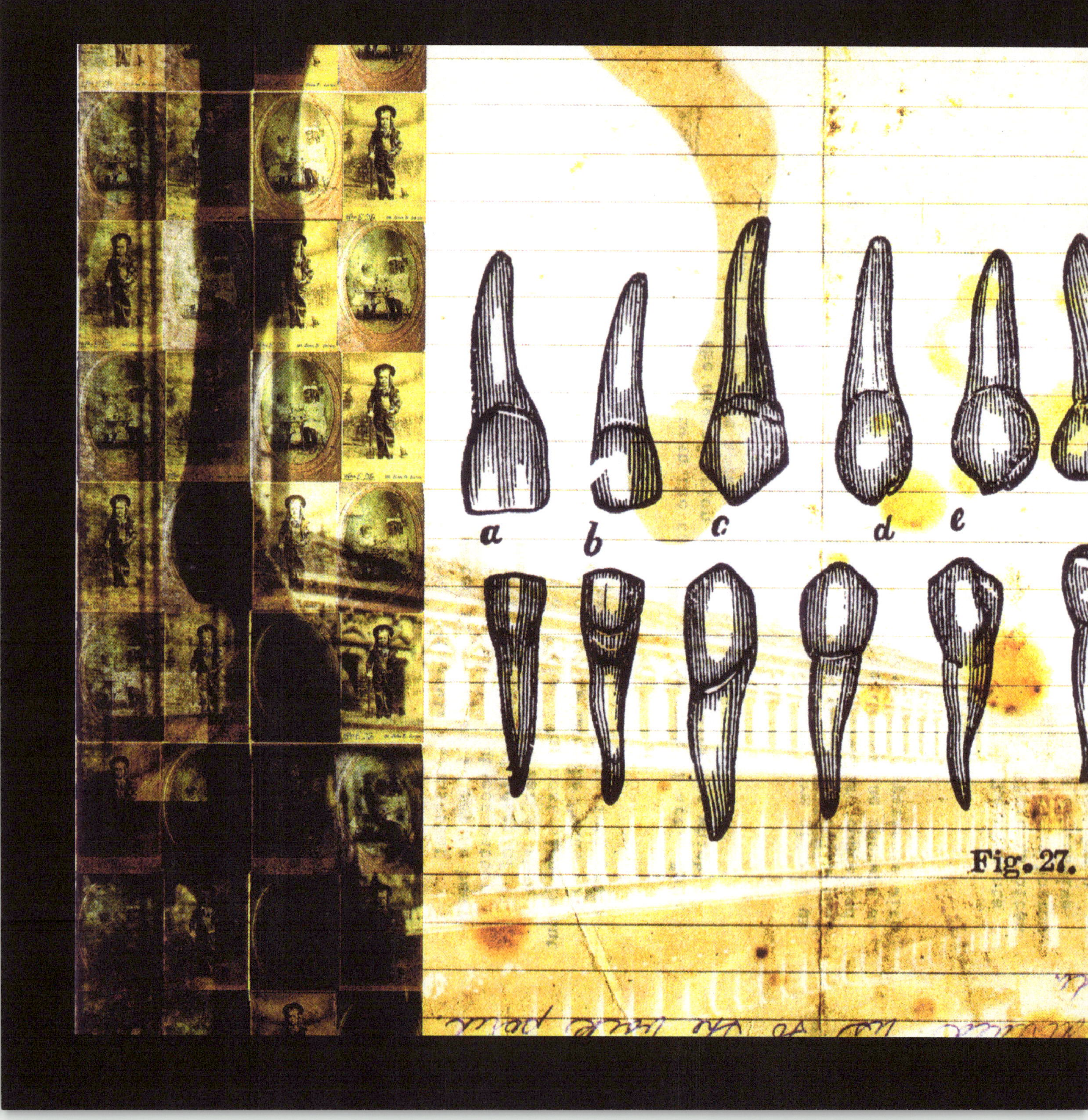
a
b
c
d
e
Fig. 27.

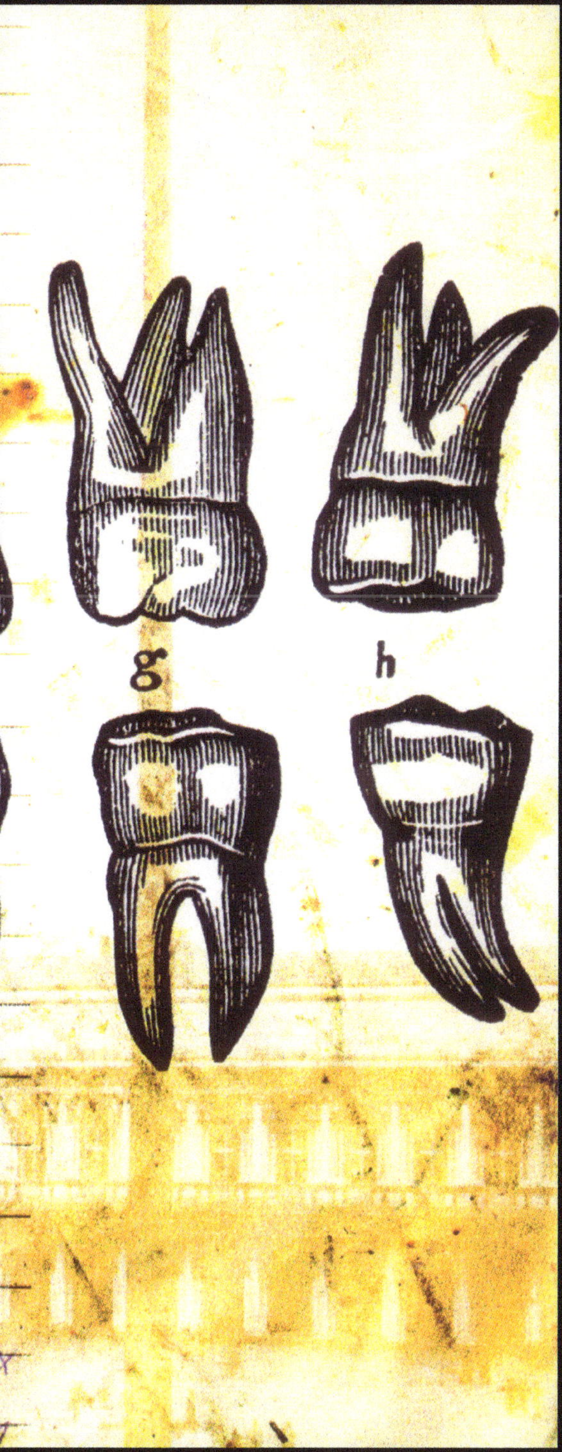
g
h

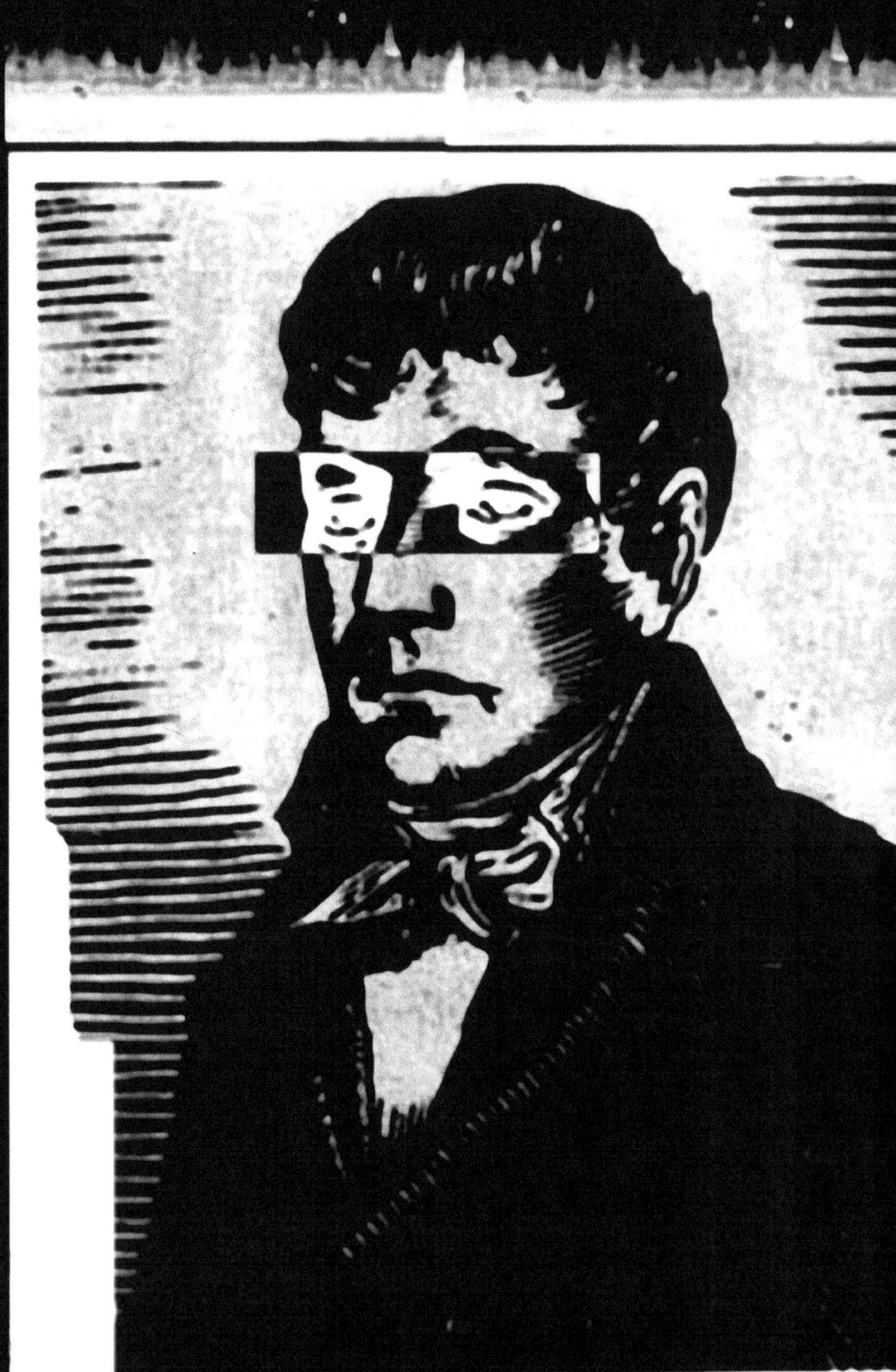

Hannibal-Rex

N

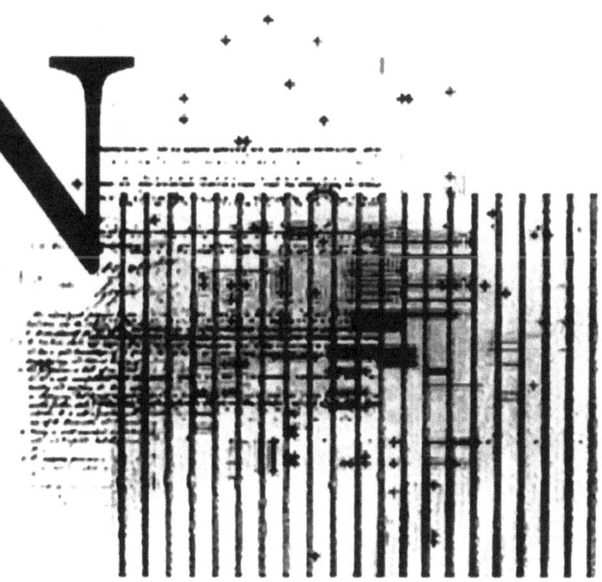

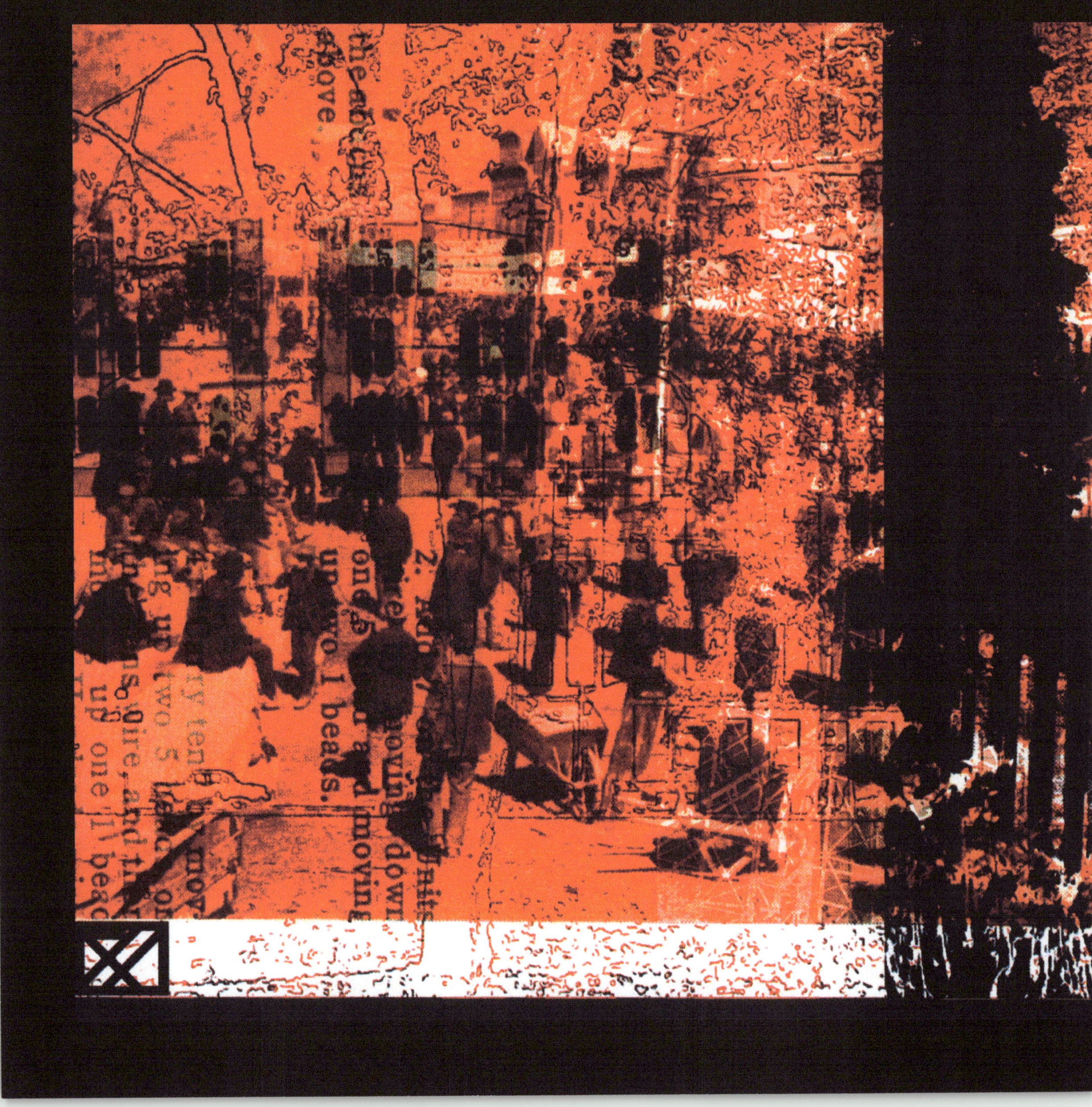

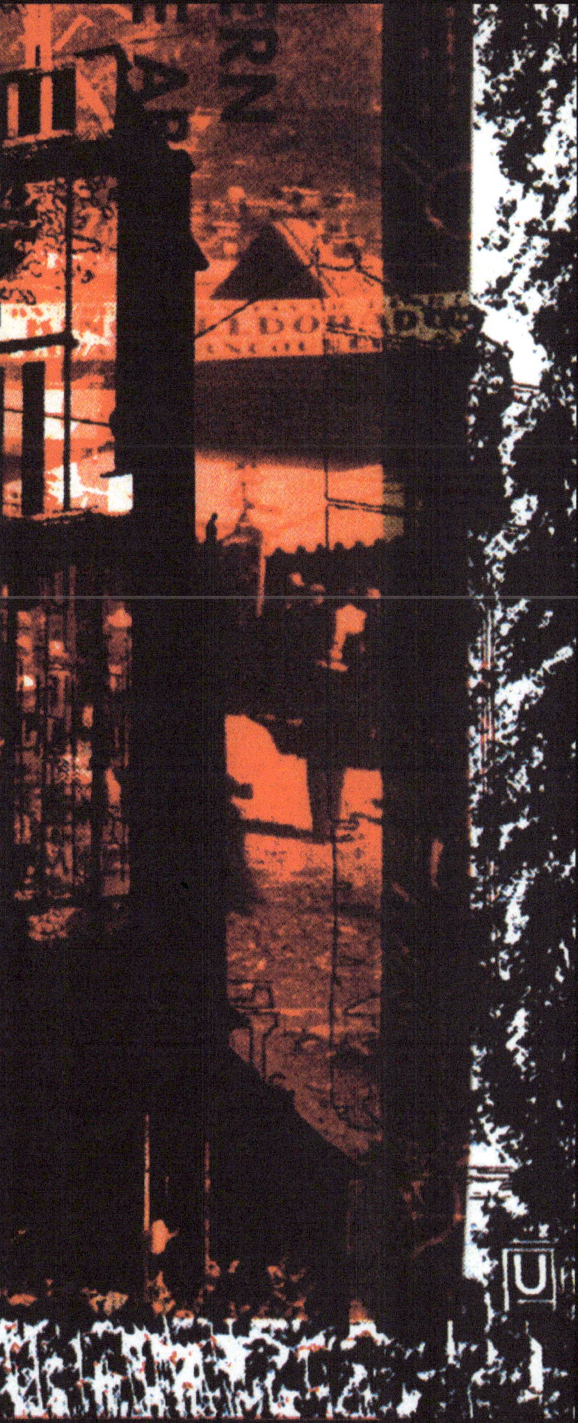

Tonight We Bleed

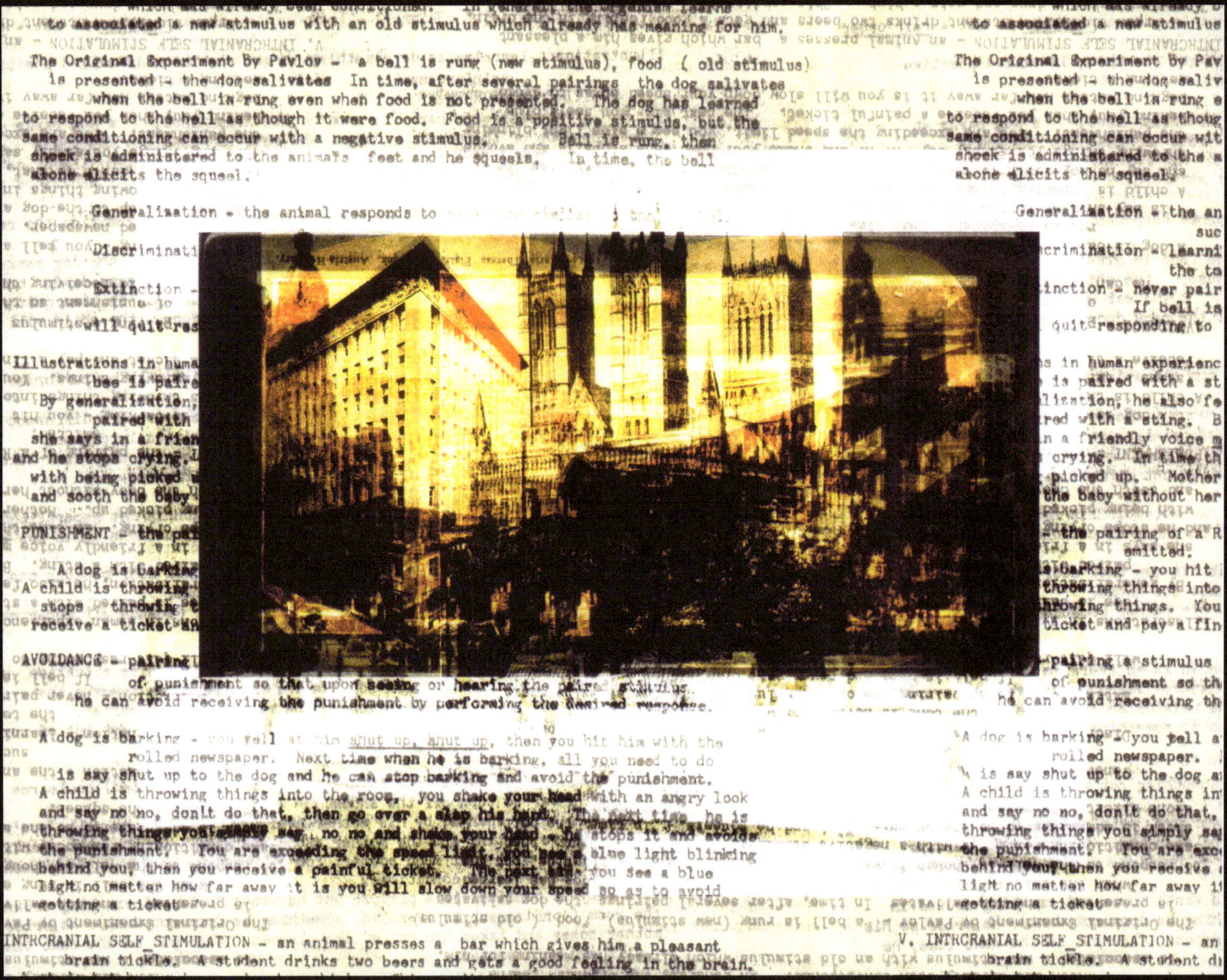

Lost-cause Factory

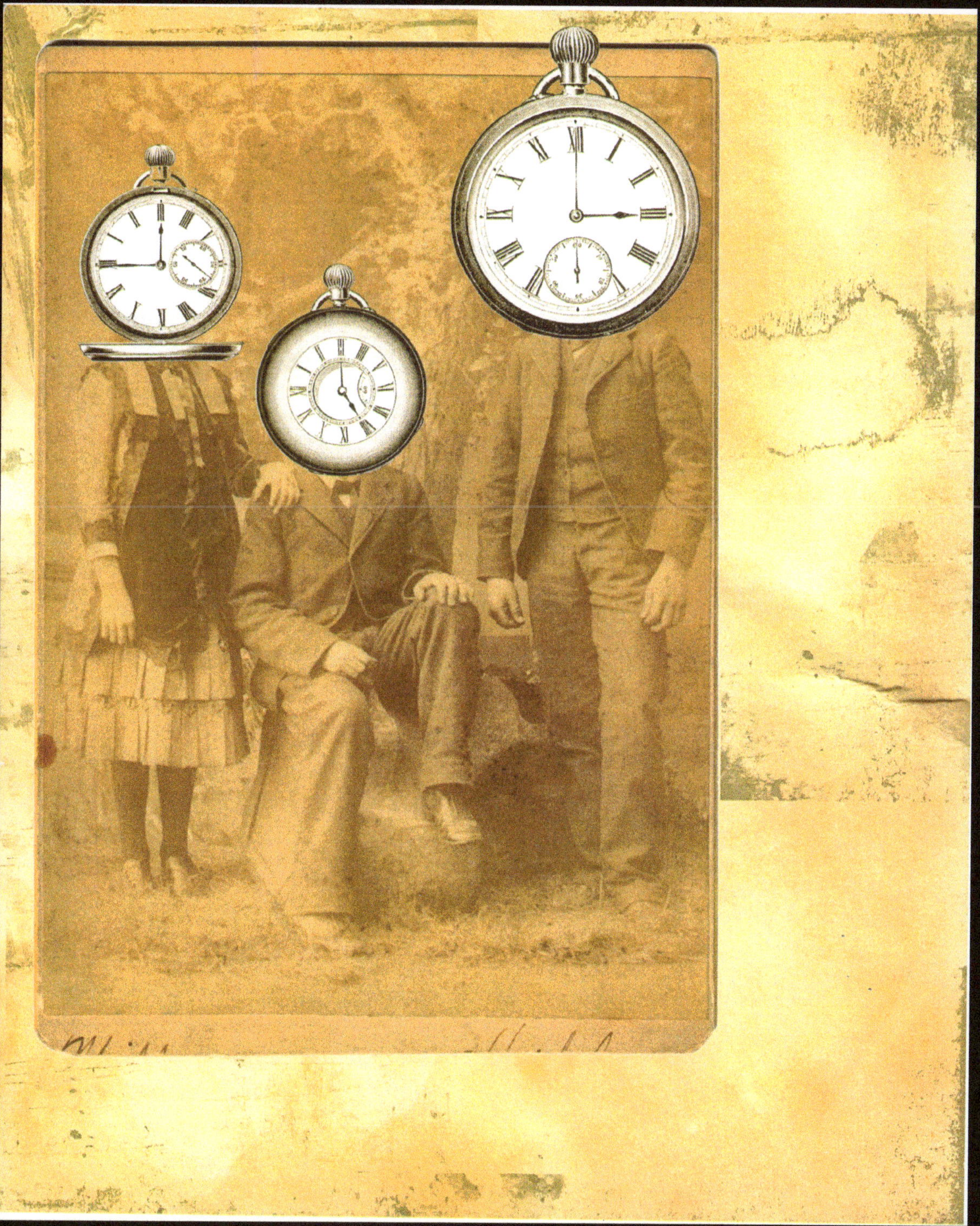

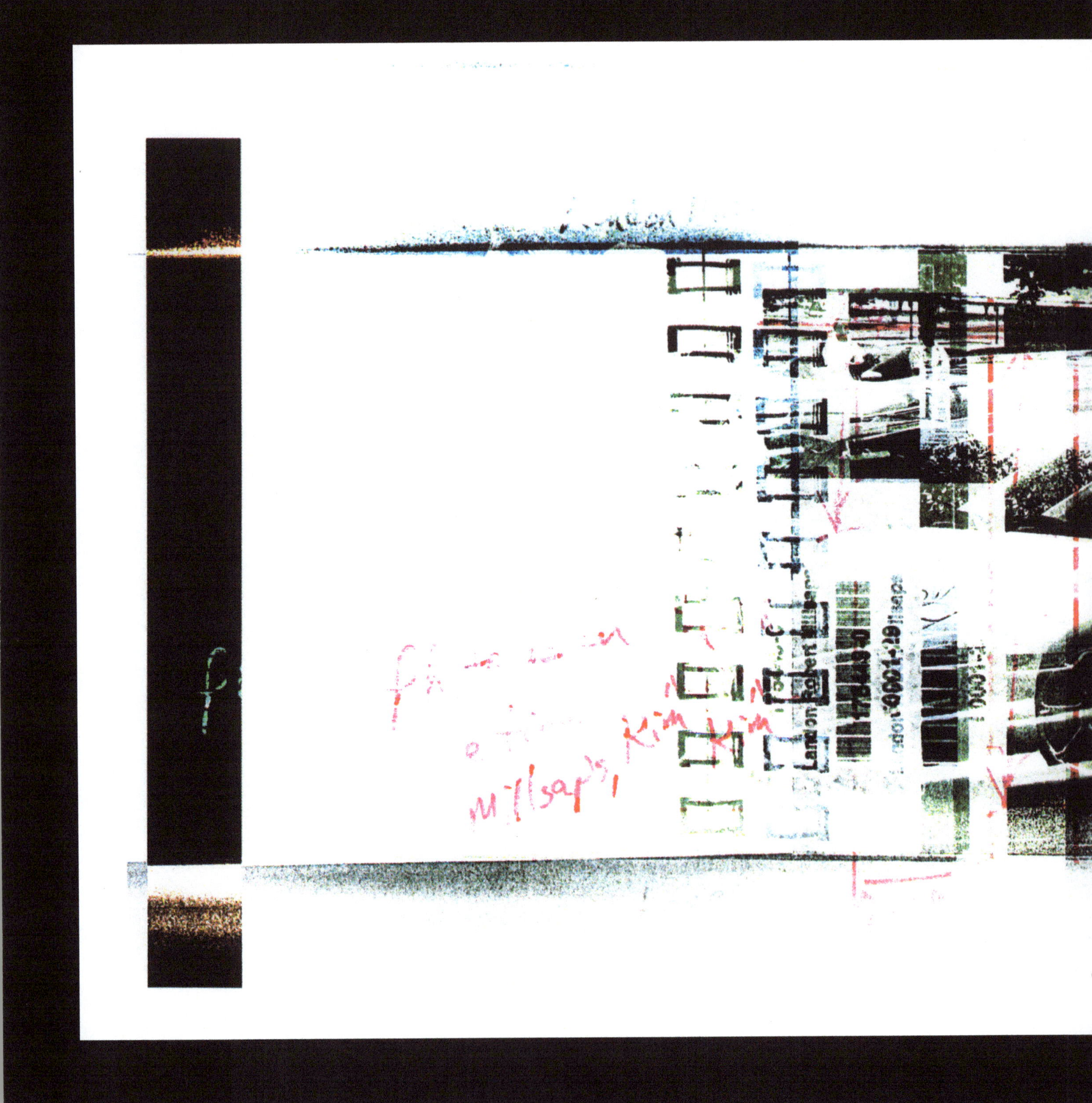
Millsaps, Kim

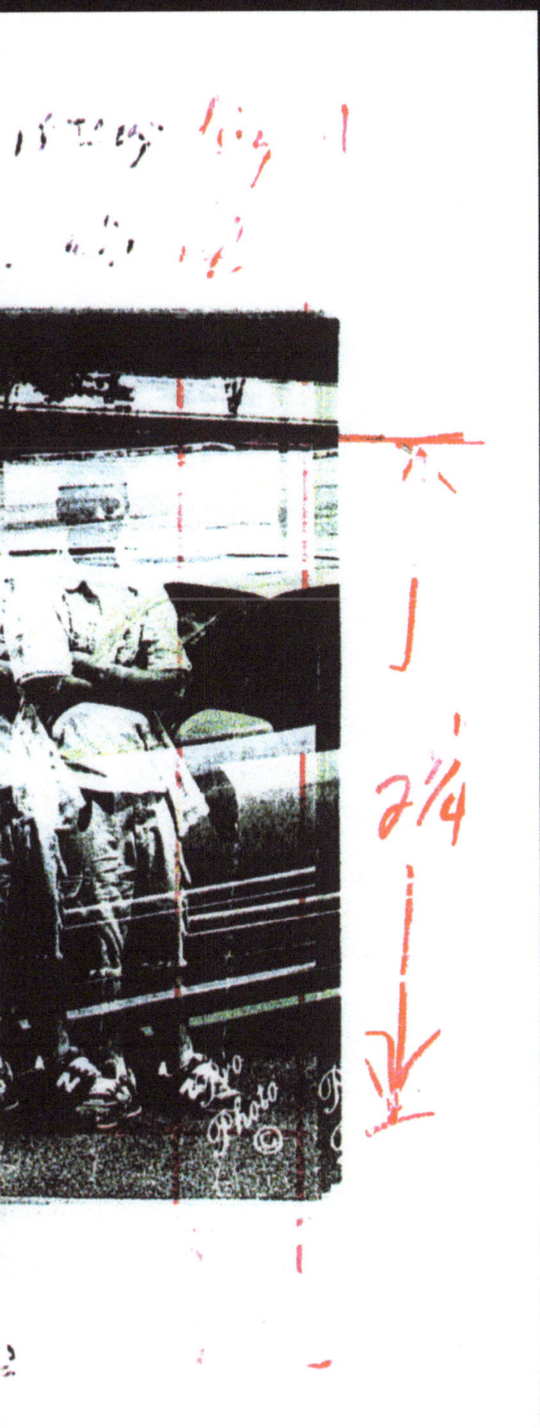

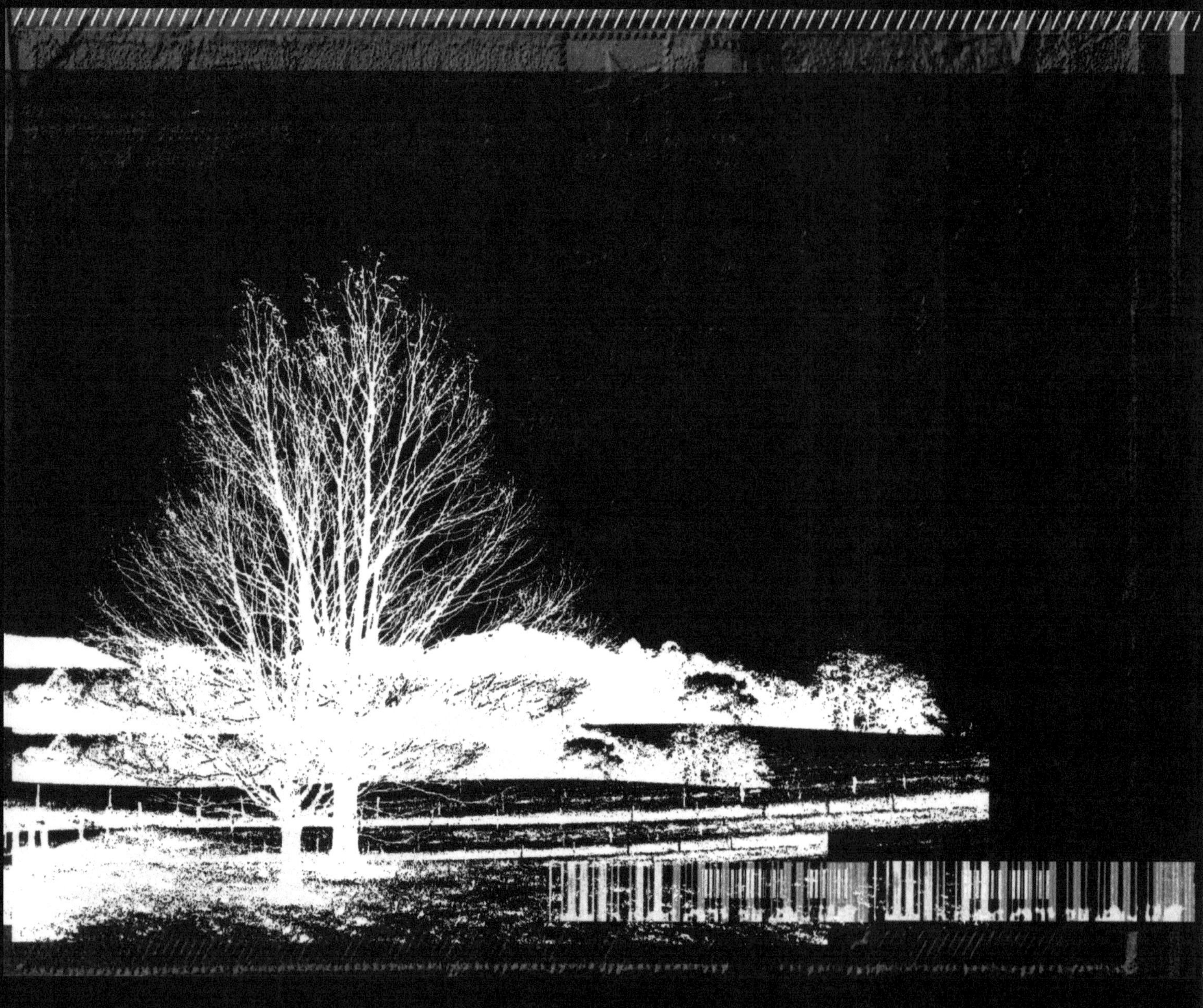

From the Museums of Sleep

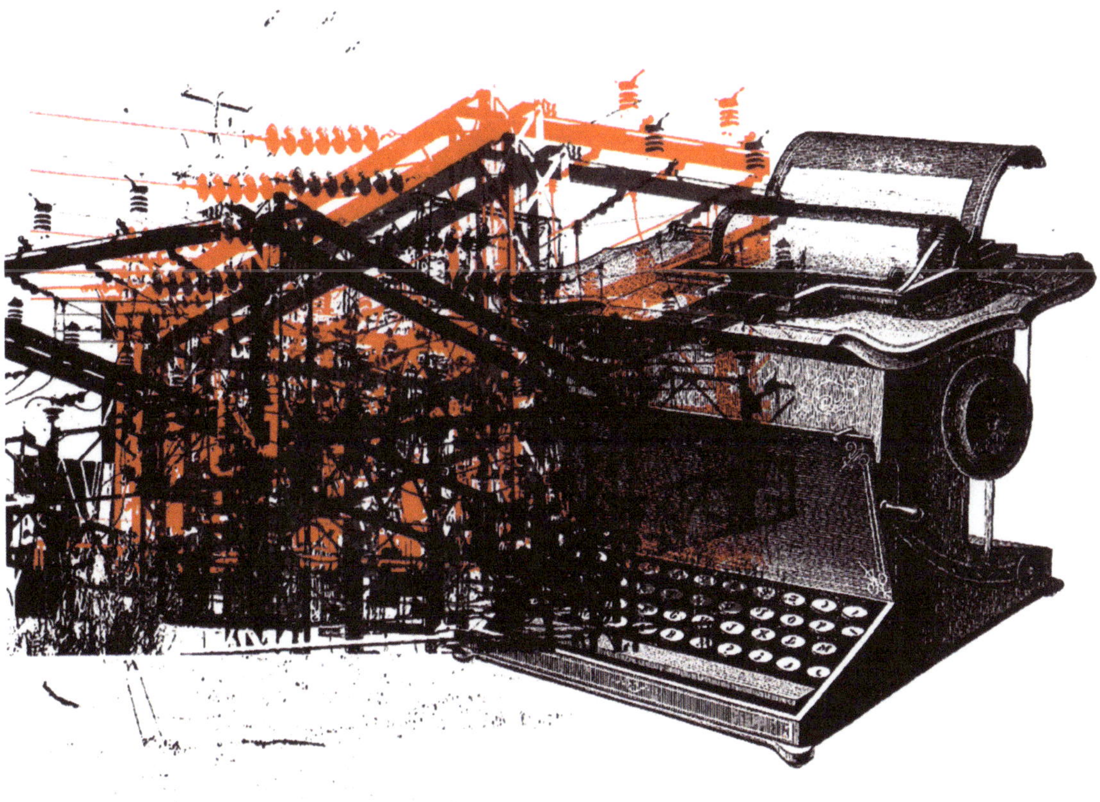

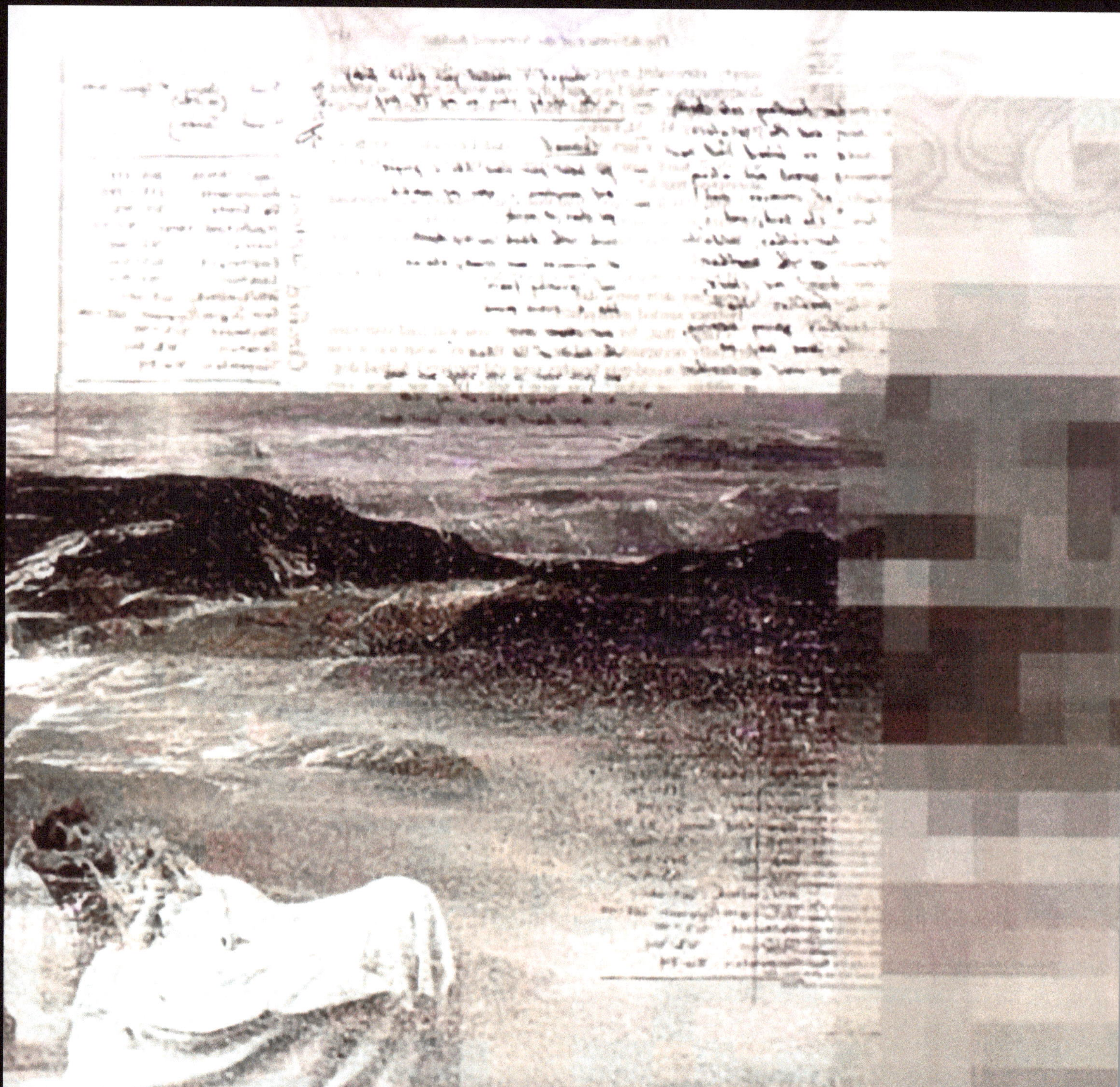

Waiting for the Ocean to Save you from the Waves

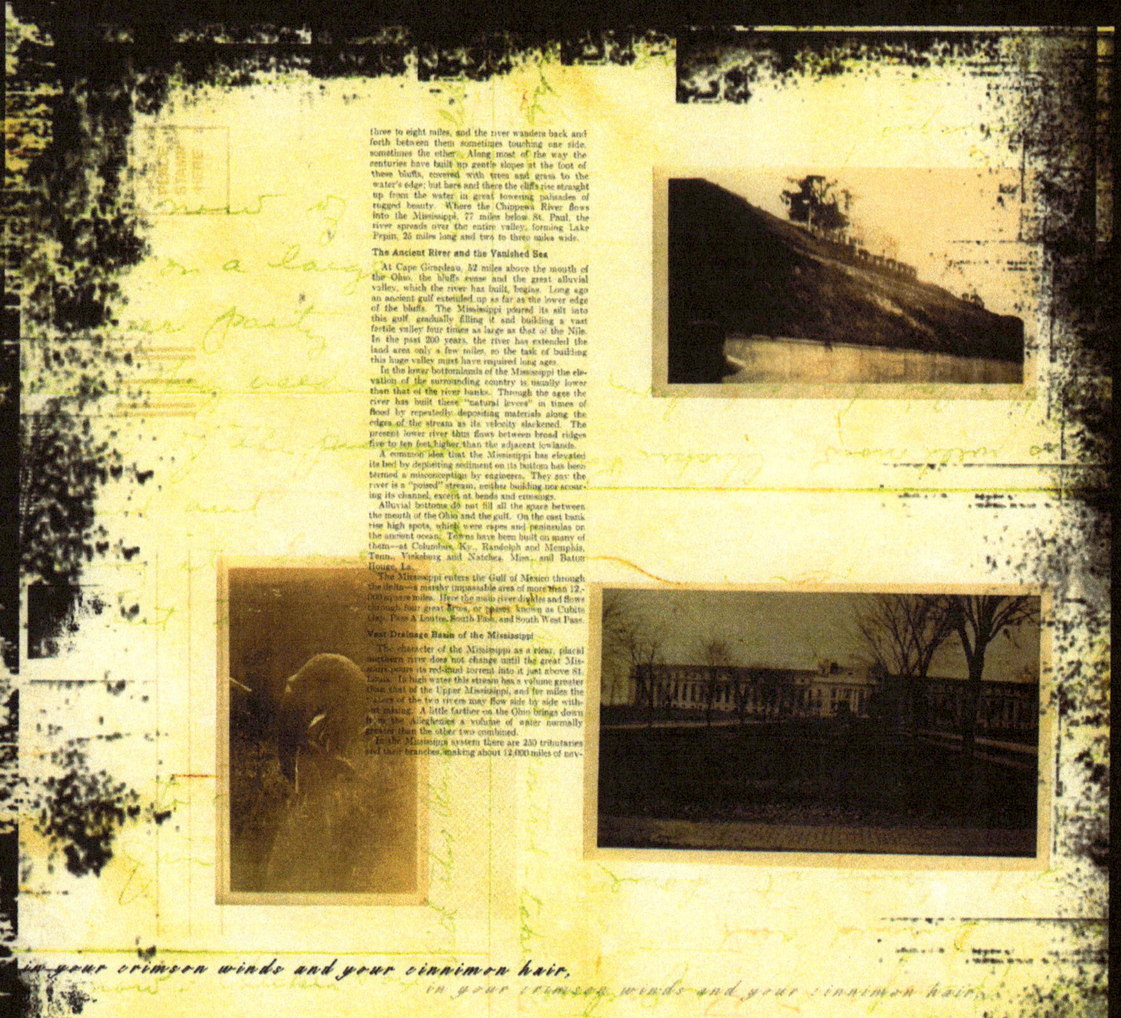

XXVI

Too much has been happening during the spring. Too many aspirations, pretensions, and boundless ambitions are hidden in its dark depths. Its expansion knows no limits. The administration of that enormous, widespread, and overgrown enterprise is sapping my strength. Wishing to share part of the burden with Rudolph, I have nominated him co-regent. Anonymously of course. Together with the stamp album we form, we three, an unofficial triumvirate, on which rests the burden of responsibility for the whole impenetrable and convoluted affair of the spring.

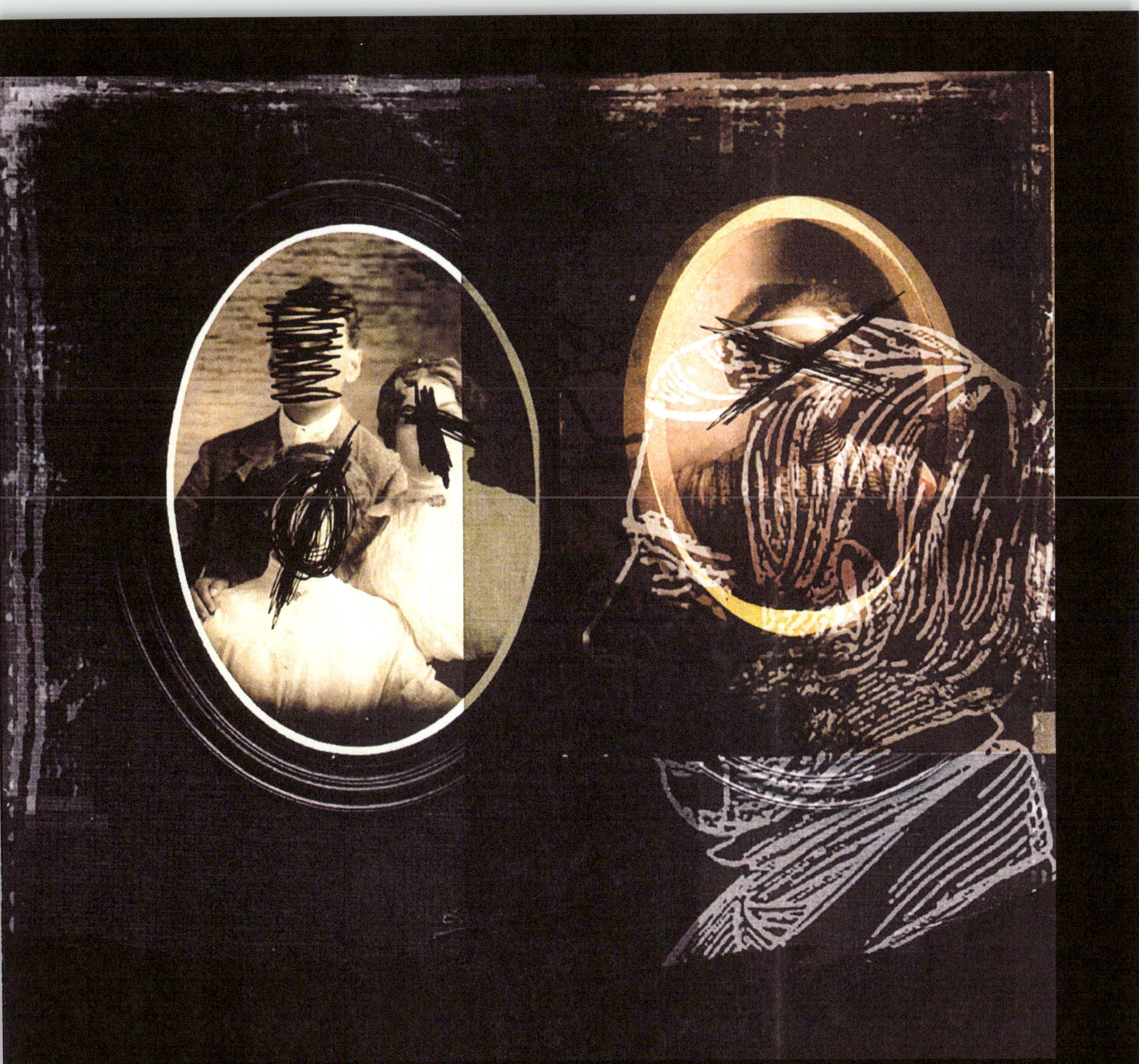

Isolation is Self-preservation

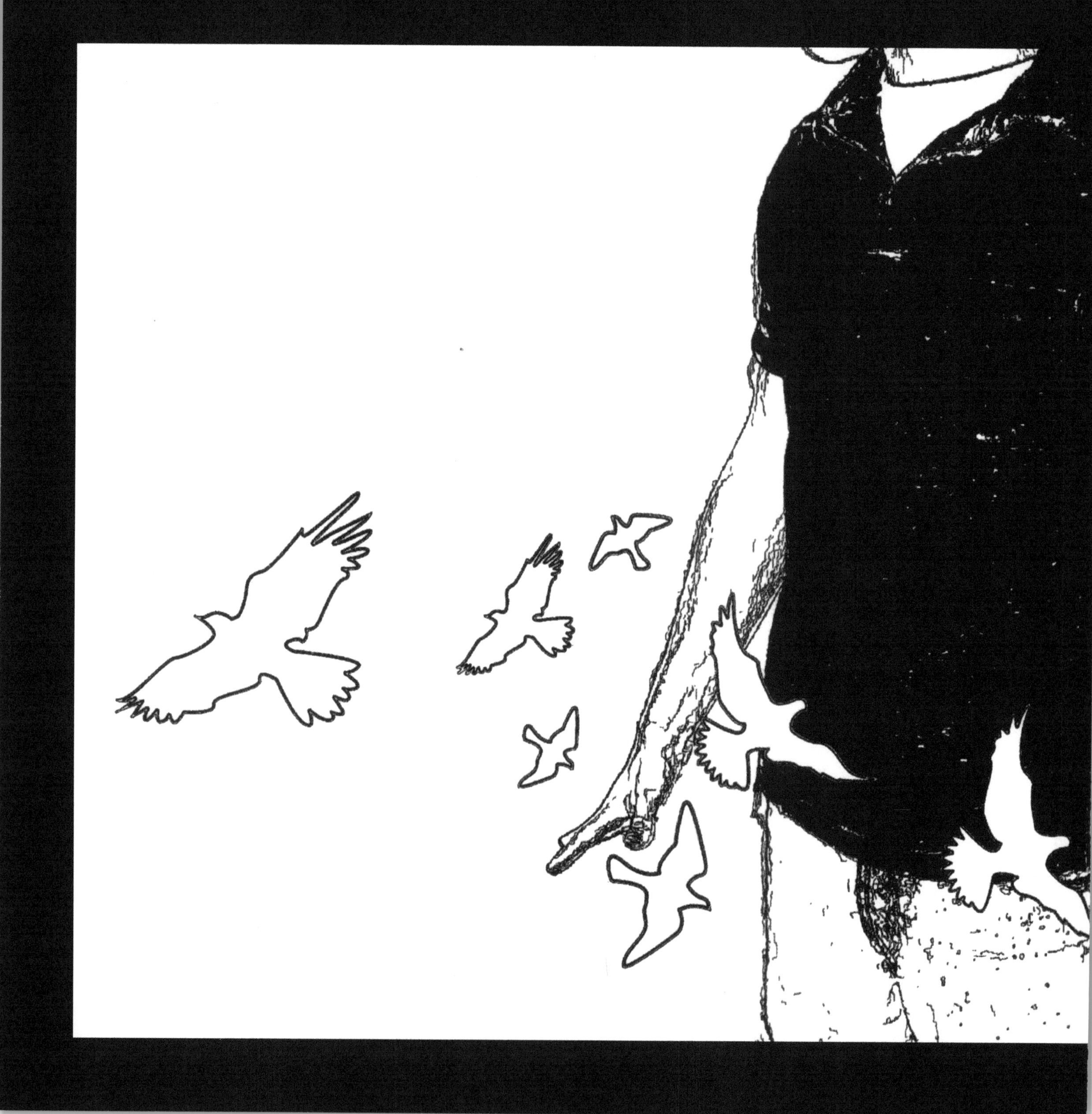

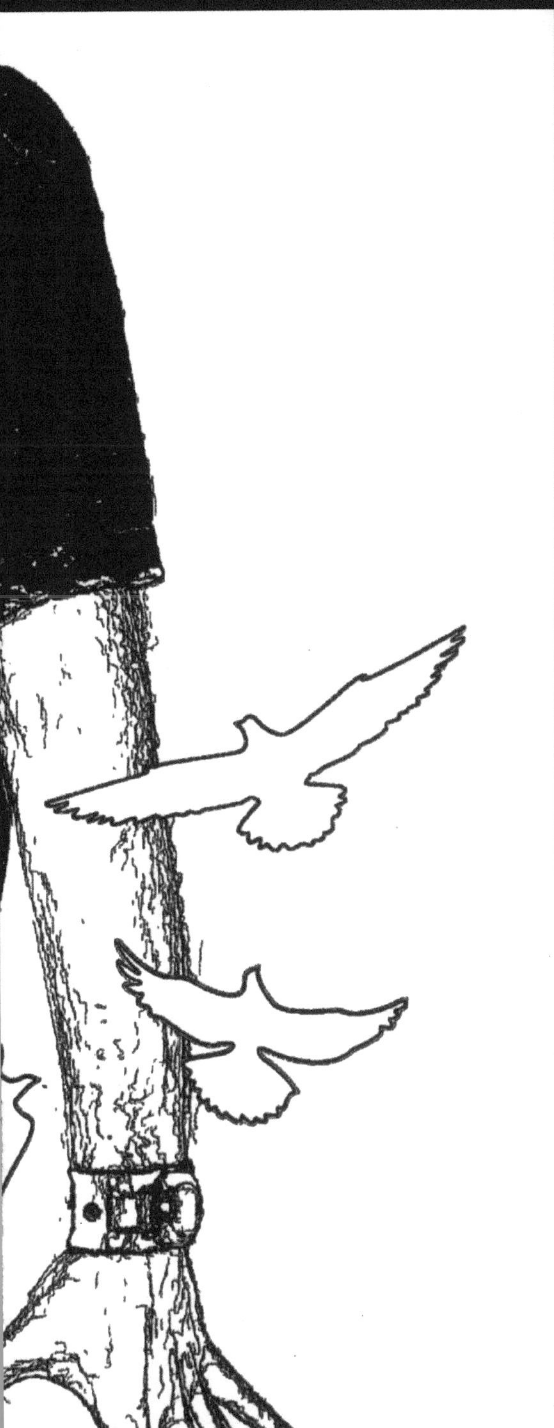

Last Stop on the Black Metal Train

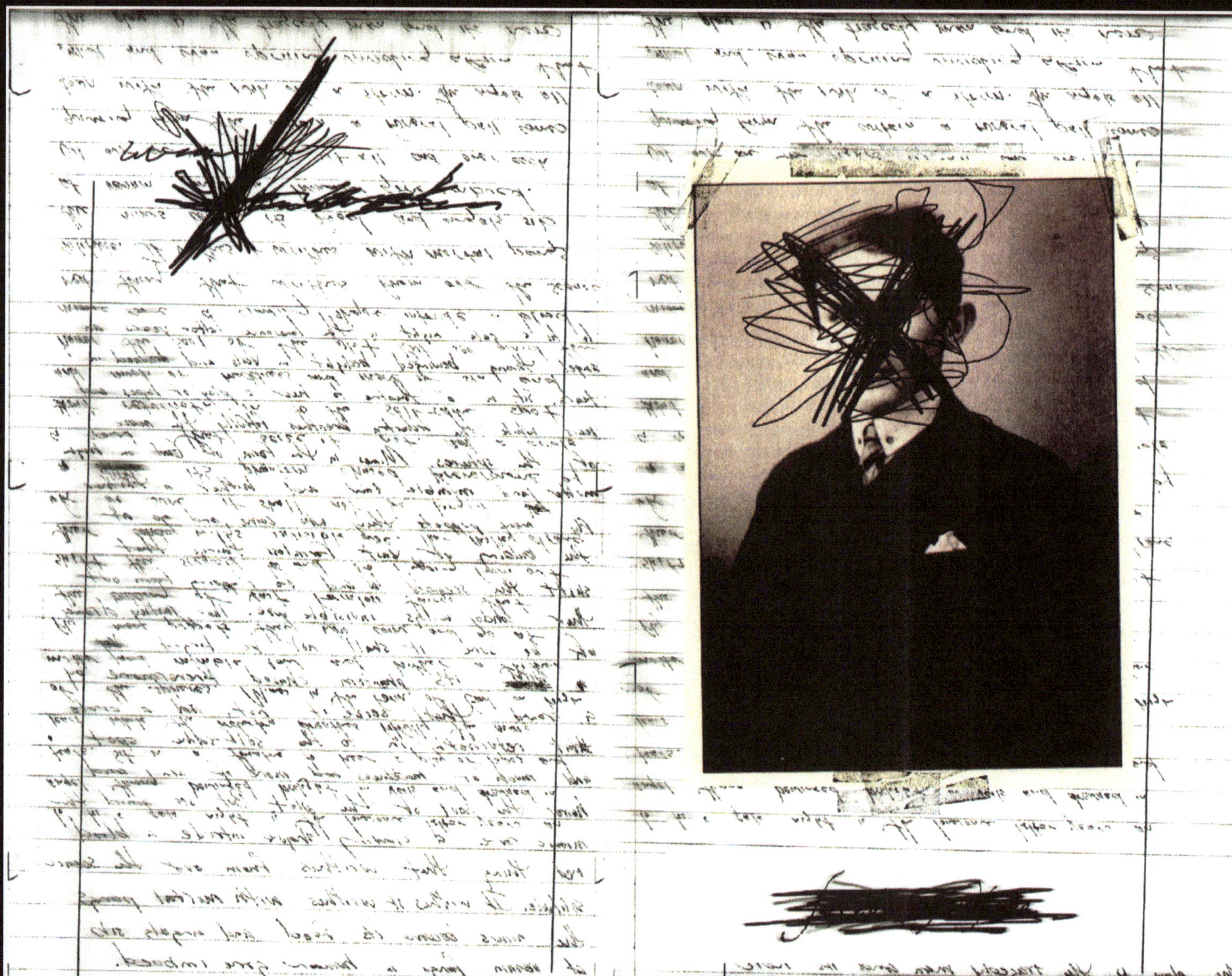

The Riddle and The Sleeping Beauty

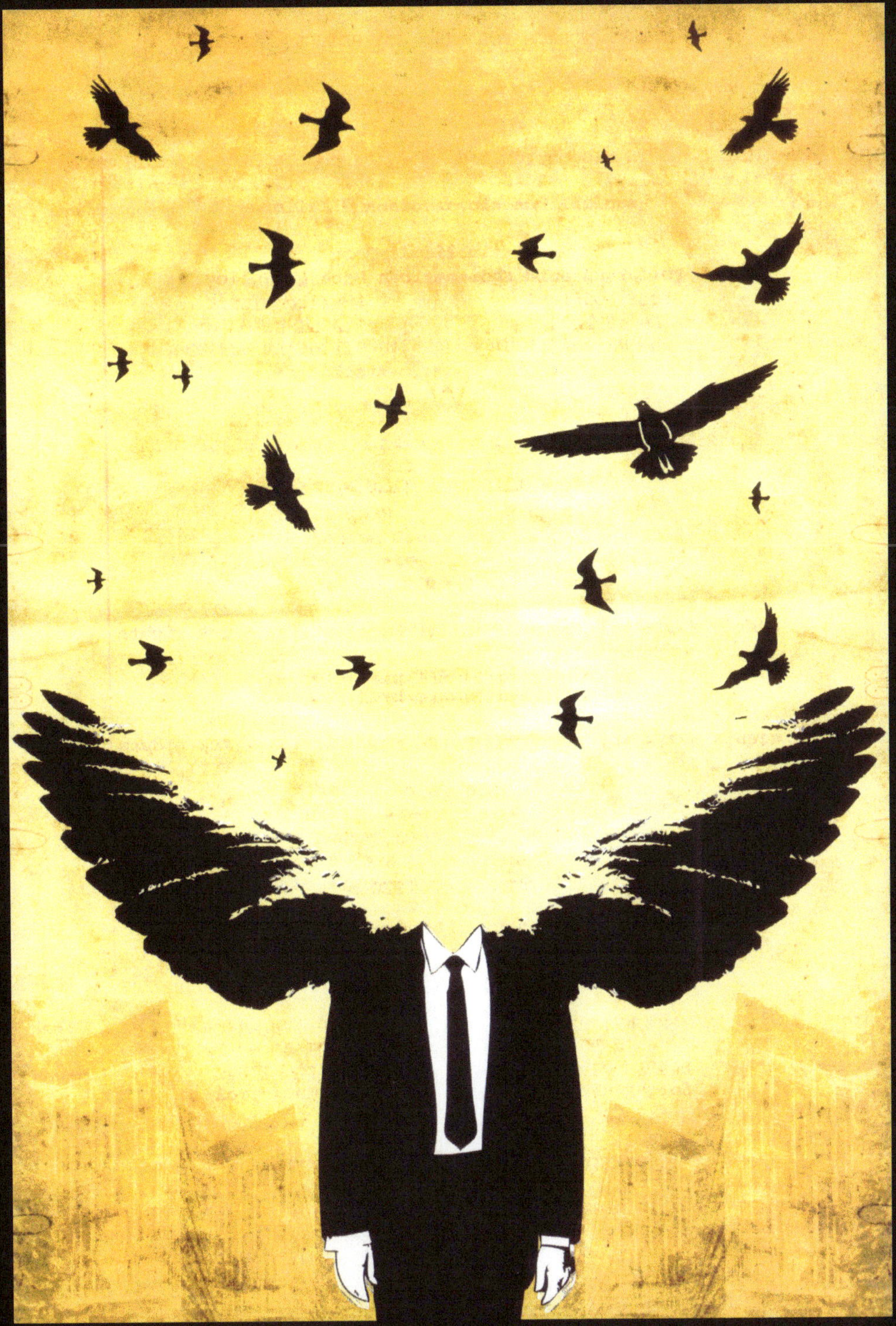

Somnambulance

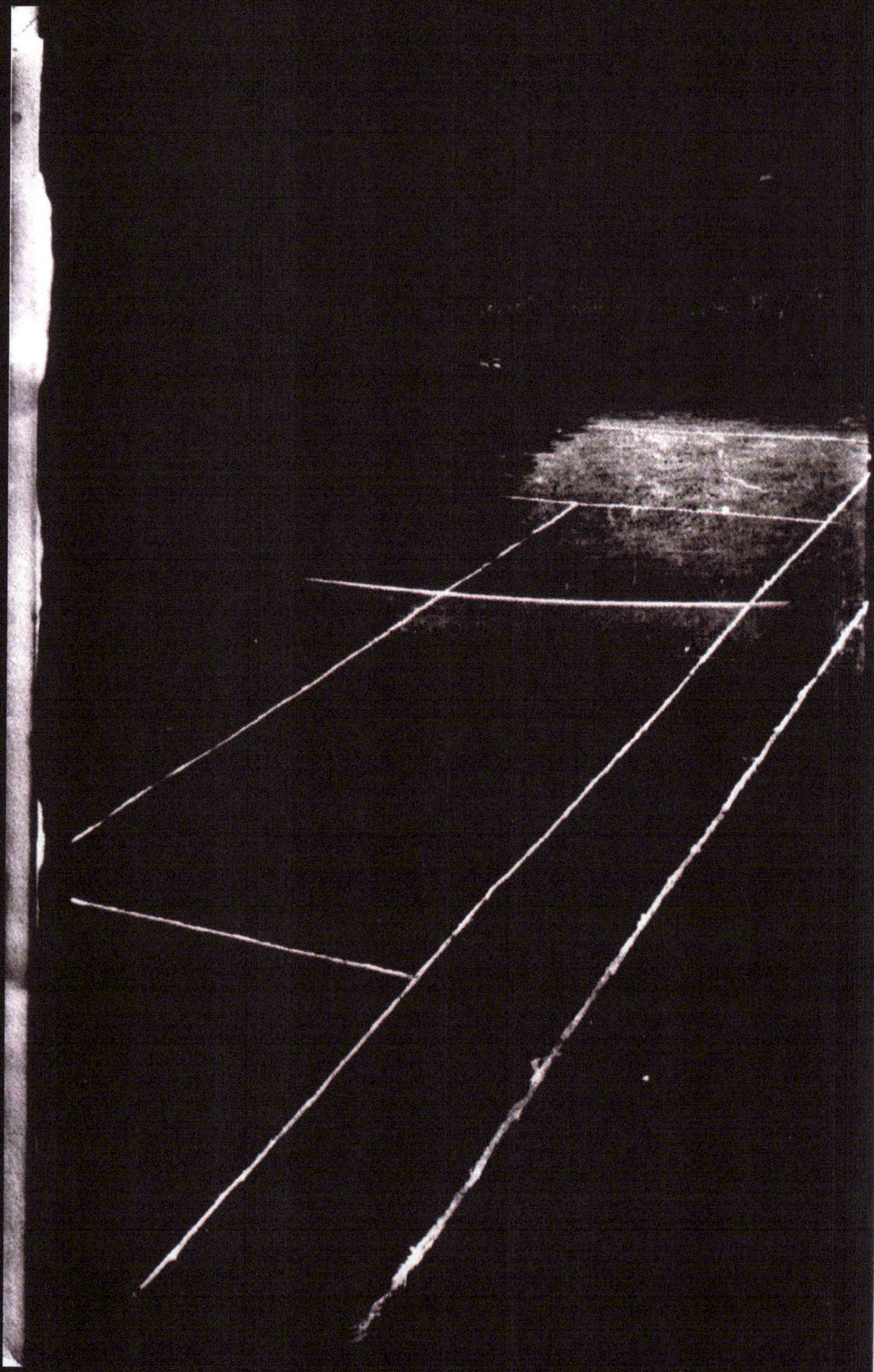

"Why, after all, should I
upright and taking norm
pavement with my stick,
of the people who pass n
entitled to complain bit
the houses like a shadow
sometimes disappearing

shamed of not walking
ps, of not tapping the
ot touching the clothes
by? Am I not rather
t having to skip along
ut a clear outline,
panes of the shipwindows?

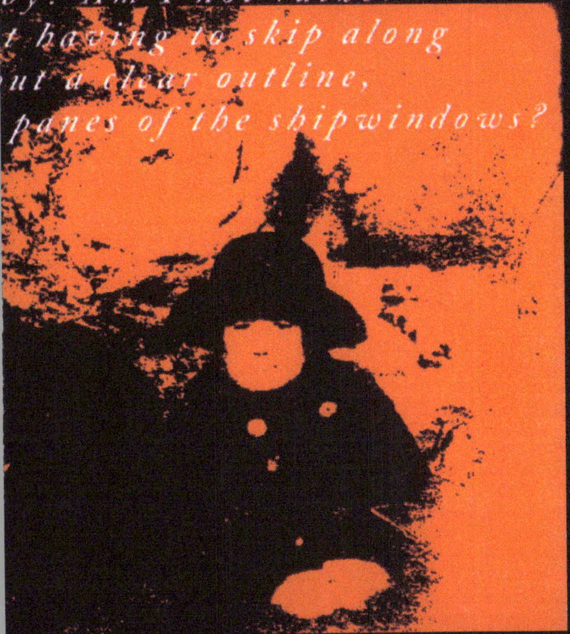

The Diplomacy of Wolves

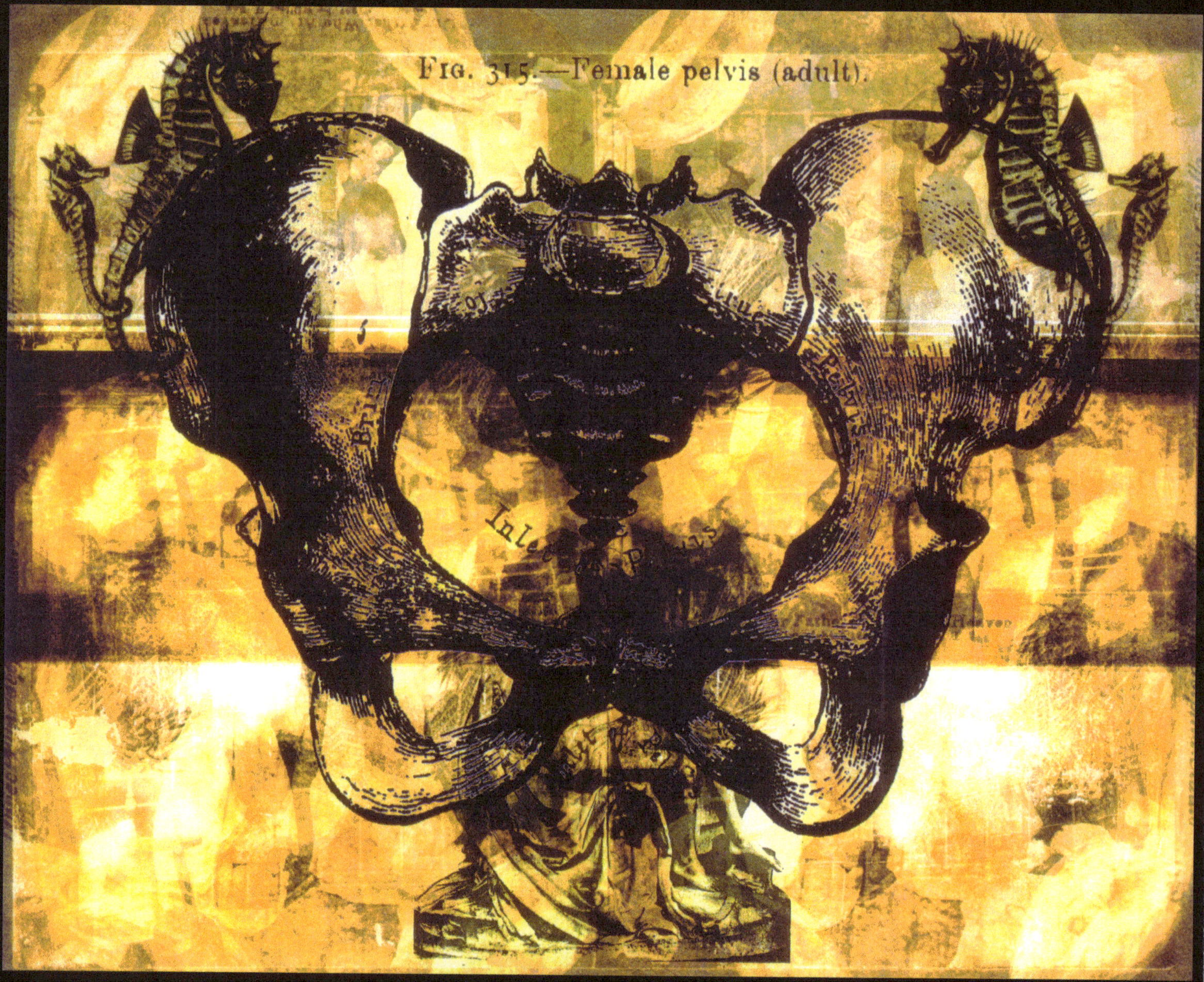

Miss Anthrophy

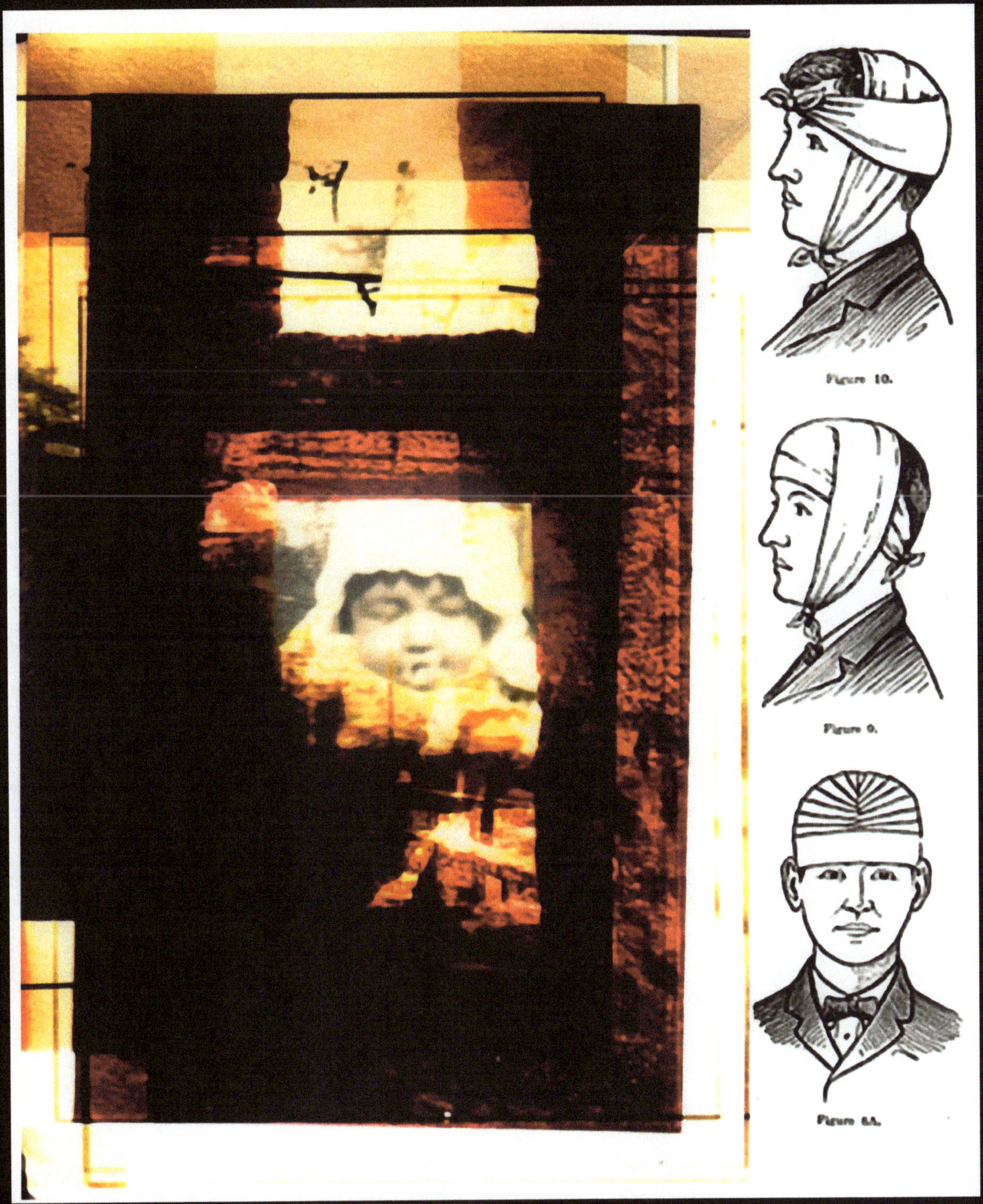
Figure 10.

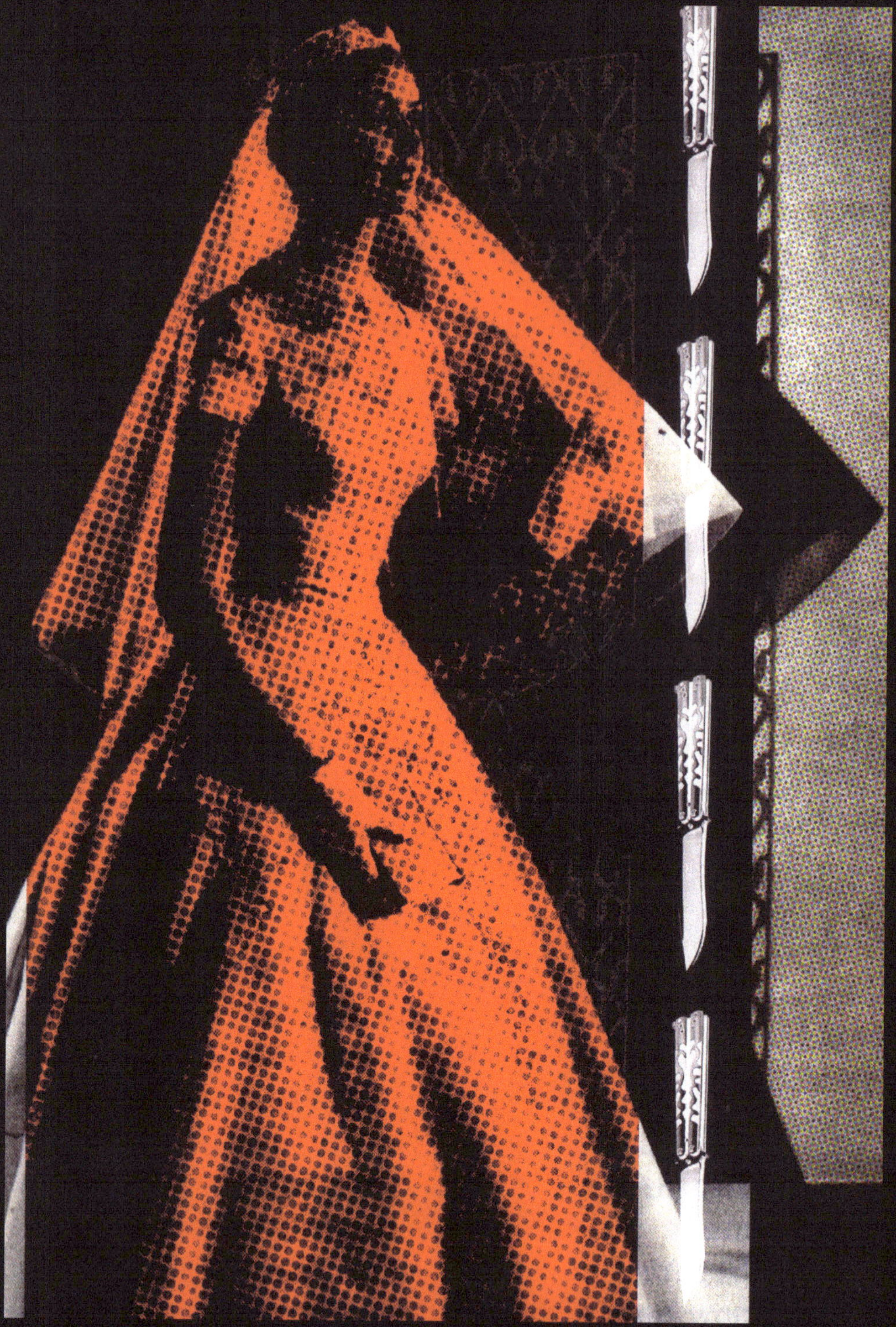

Sex is the New Violence

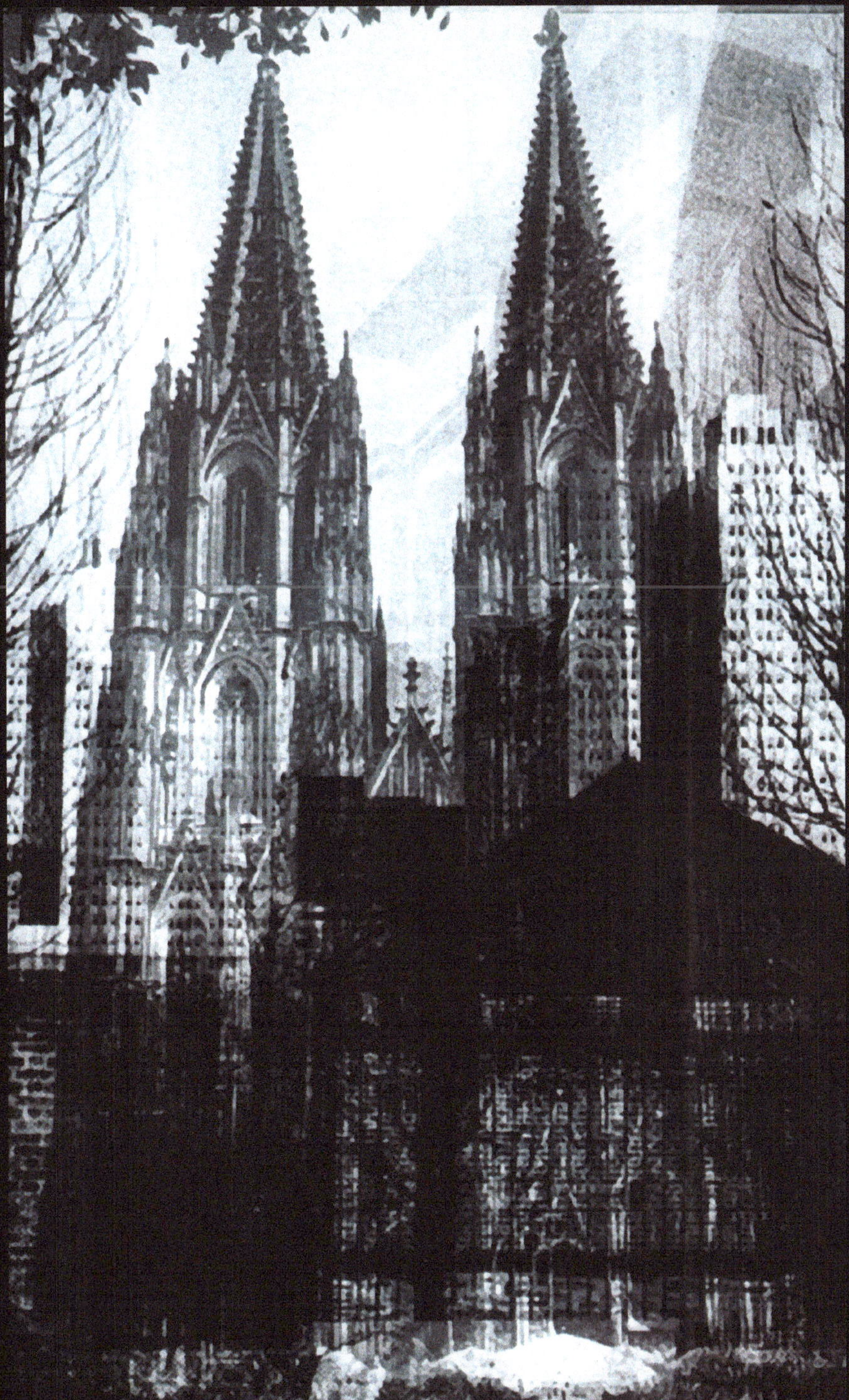

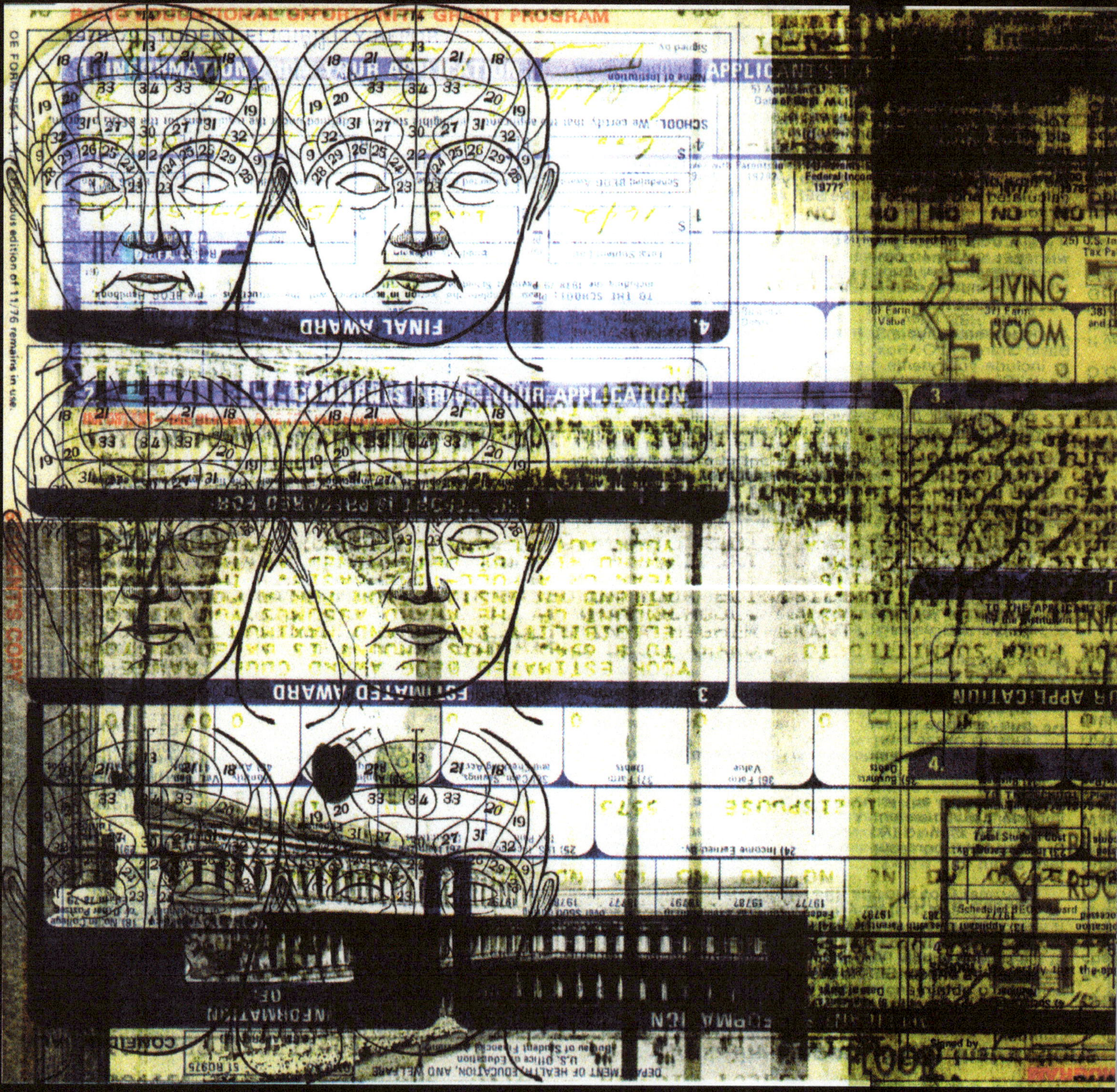

GRANT PROGRAM
FINAL AWARD
ESTIMATED AWARD
LIVING
ROOM

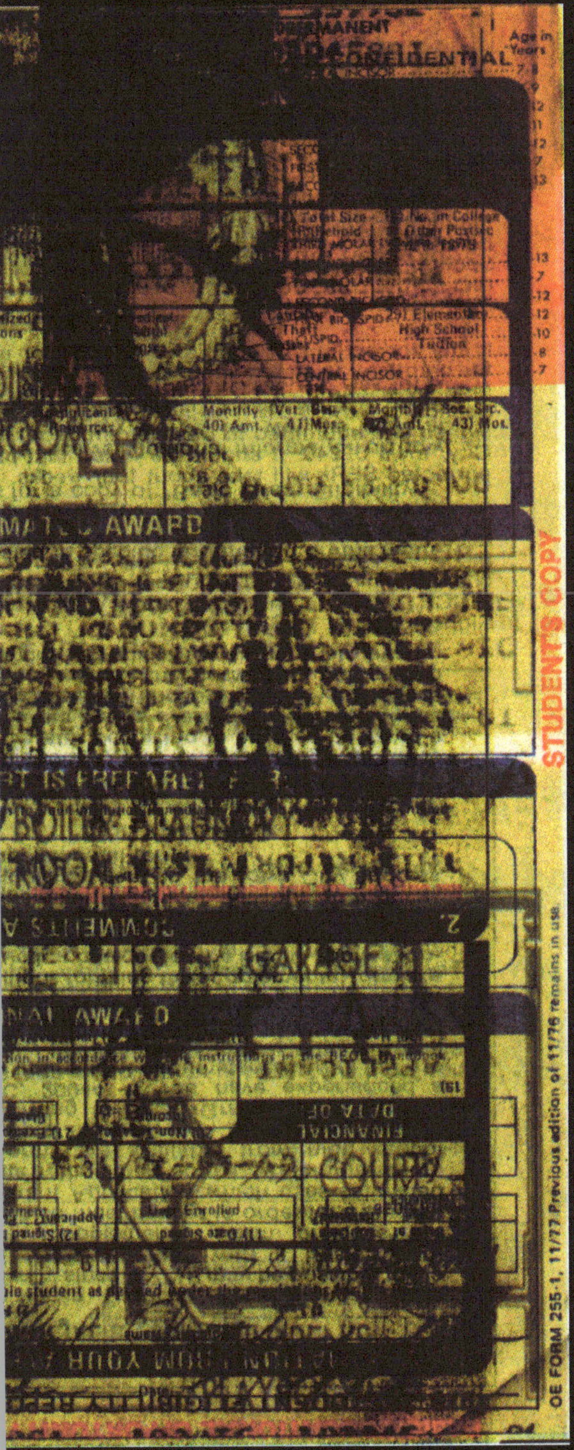

CONFIDENTIAL
STUDENT'S COPY
OE FORM 255-1, 11/77 Previous edition of 11/76 remains in use.

Isaiah

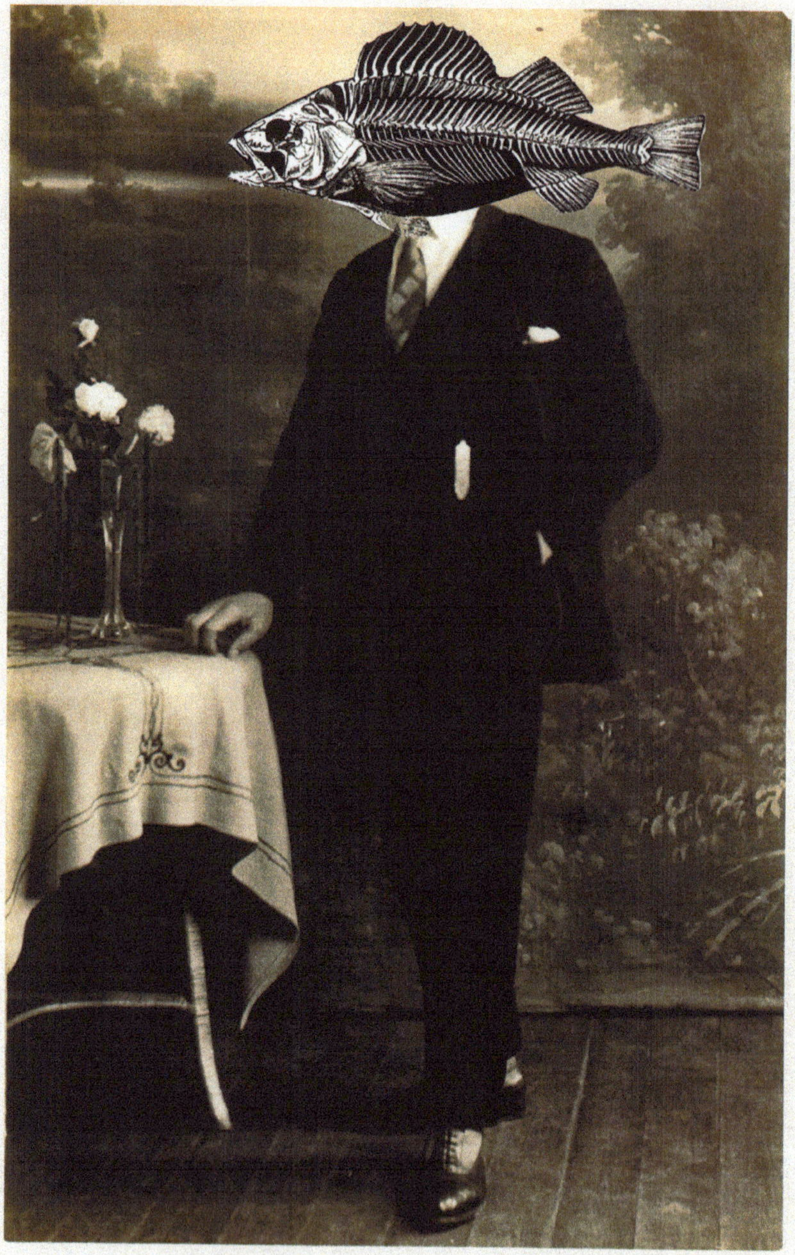

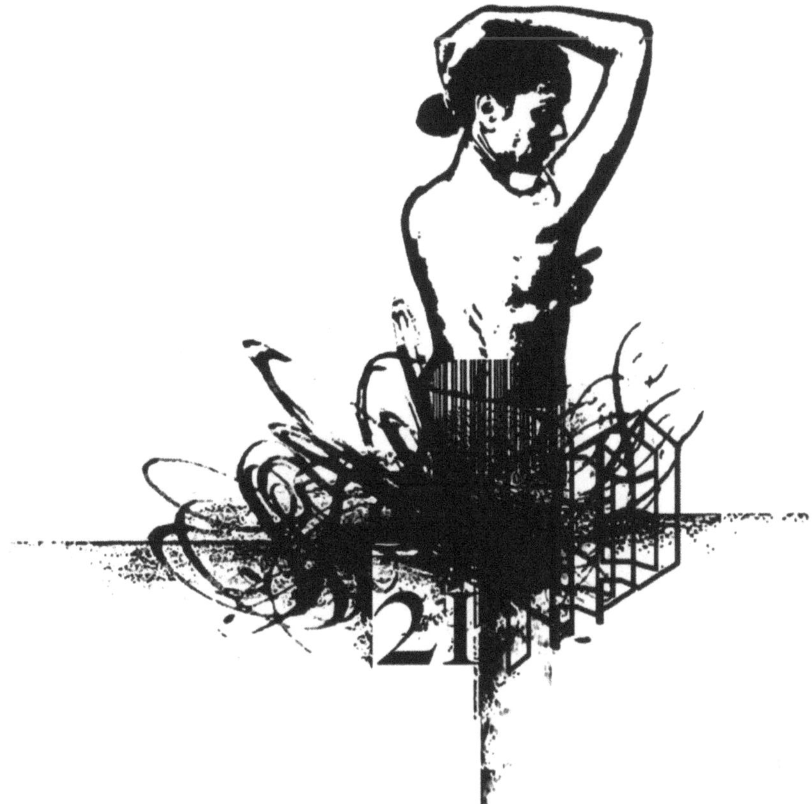

21

"I usually wind up in a cemetery."

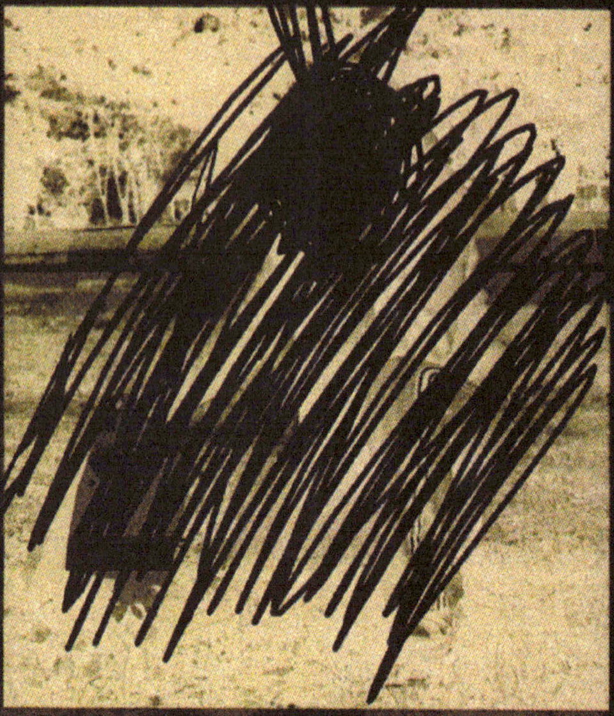

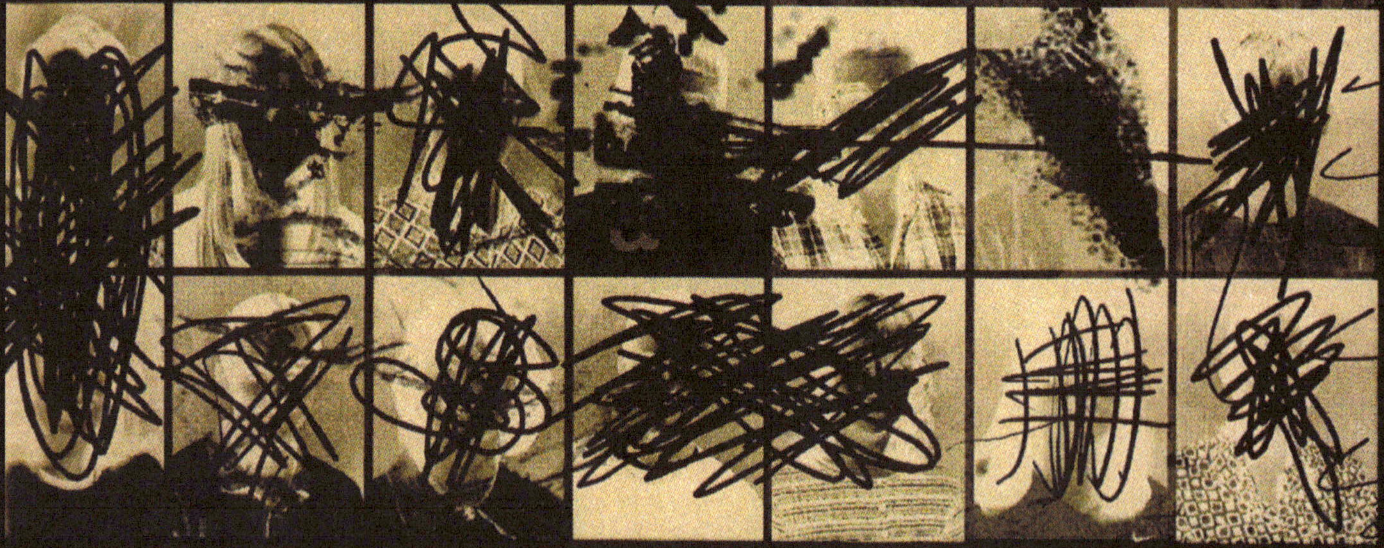

After f
stone ru
Grindle
lookin
graves w
are any
esting g
trace. G
out goin
ies to ha
of peac
quietnes
goes qu
so she c
esting st
old Gates
stones.

L. T.
Ashle
Shaun
Mitc
Ran
Chri
Jas

Je
join
Trena
ChrisJ
Mo
Deea
Cry

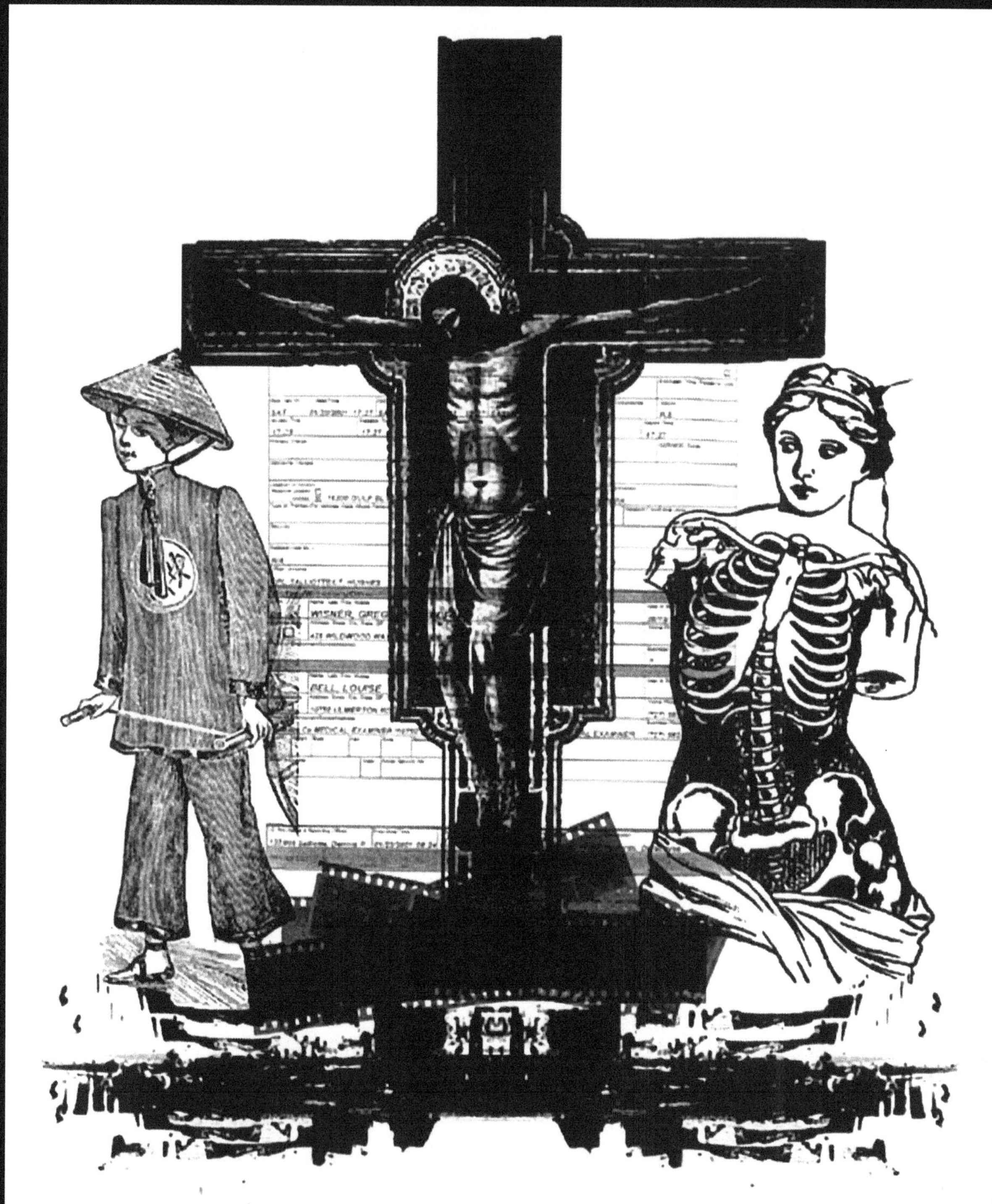
WISNER, GREG
BELL, LOUISE

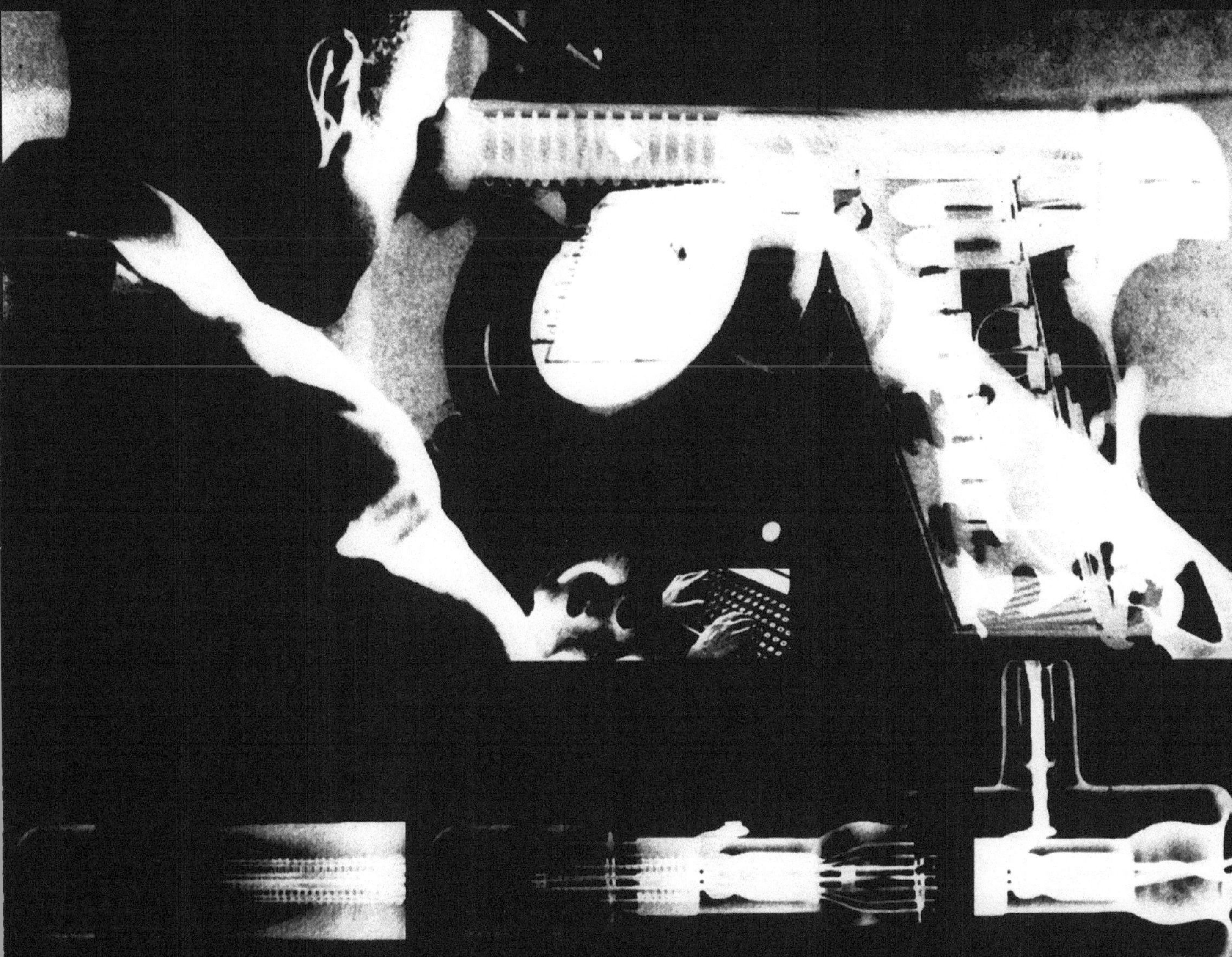

Your Scene is Dead

www.ingramcontent.com/pod-product-compliance
Lightning Source LLC
Chambersburg PA
CBHW042026200526
45172CB00028B/1124
9781090489197